PINBALL

GARY FLOWER

& BILL KURTZ

CHARTWELL
BOOKS, INC.

A QUINTET BOOK

Published by Chartwell Books
A Division of Book Sales, Inc.
110 Enterprise Avenue
Secaucus, New Jersey 07094

ISBN 1-55521-322-7

This book was designed and produced by
Quintet Publishing Limited
6 Blundell Street
London N7 9BH

Design Director: Peter Bridgewater
Art Director: Ian Hunt
Designer: Helen White
Editors: Ag MacKeith, Shaun Barrington

Typeset in Great Britain by
Central Southern Typesetters, Eastbourne
Manufactured in Hong Kong by
Regent Publishing Services Limited
Printed in Hong Kong by
South Sea Int'l Press Ltd.

DEDICATION

This book is dedicated to

Betty, for yesterday, today and tomorrow
JH who brought music to my ears
Wayne Neyens for Square Head
Harry Williams whom I have never met but have a lot
to be grateful for
Norm Clark for Magic City
Steve Kordek for keeping the pinball torch alive.

CONTENTS

INTRODUCTION

This book presents a history of pinball from its beginnings in the 1930s, when the machines were little more than coin-operated bagatelle games, to the complex microelectronics offered today. The skills of the graphic artists are displayed, and the technical innovations are charted, from the forties mechanical flipper to the eighties machine that talks back.

One of the themes developed is, in fact, how pinball games are always at the forefront of technology because they have consistently capitalized on the latest development before it permeates into other areas. Thus the microchip – with such widespread application in the last quarter of the 20th century – was part of pinball machinery when universal microchip-based calculators were still a glint in the eye of the computer whizz kids.

Pinball art has always reflected topical events. Witness the preponderance of space games in the sixties when the space race was a global obsession. In the same way, celebrity-linked games, a phenomenon of the seventies which portrayed people like Dolly Parton, Elton John, Muhammed Ali (and of course Roger Daltrey from the rock opera 'Tommy', about the curative powers of the silver ball) act as a kind of sub-cultural register of contemporary fashions and outlook.

Other games have plugged into TV and the cinema – *Star Trek*, *The Pink Panther*, *Flash Gordon*. Comic book heroes like Flash, such as Superman and Spiderman, have been decorating backglasses for decades. And the video game boom inevitably affected pinball – but did not destroy it – as machines began to feed off the success of *Space Invaders*, *Defender* and *Quest* by using the same names and images.

Most pinball machines are designed and built in Chicago: but was it always the pinball capital of the world? The answer is in Chapter Seven, where the European contribution is appraised, and where also one of the classic games of the sixties is examined in detail by Dan Kramer, an authority on games of that era. We hope that this book will inform both the pinball fanatics – the collectors and competitors – and the casual player. Lights. Action. Roll 'em.

LEFT *Detail of the playfield of
Bally's* Medusa, *which featured a
bonus bar for extended play.*

ABOVE *Gottlieb's* Gigi *(1964);
thank 'eavens for little girls.*

THE LURE OF THE SILVERBALL

Who plays pinball? There is no simple answer. We all recognize the stereotype, The Fonz character: archetypal 1950s rock'n'roller, leather jacket, jeans and T-shirt, slicked-back hair and the motorcycle outside. Maybe that was a true picture thirty years ago, but somehow I suspect it reflects more cinematic romance than reality.

In the thirties pinball's biggest fans were the unemployed, who found it a cheap and novel form of entertainment. Today the players may be tycoons who have the latest machine in their penthouses, families who have one in the den, collectors who hanker for a bygone era, or perhaps technicians who get their fun messing about inside the machine, rather than playing the game; and of course a whole army of marauding vacationers who get their only exposure to these machines when they invade the shore.

Then there are the casual players, like the guy who chances on a pintable in a bar or the kid who decides to check out the old-tech machines now he no longer gets the same thrill from the video games he has grown up with; either may go on to become a pinball junkie.

It is no accident that I refer to the pinball player as "he." The typical player is male. The reason for this has more to do with culture than ability. Pinball games are essentially designed by men for men to play. The themes of the games relate to the macho male ideal. Recurrent themes for these machines include card games and pool, for example.

You might think, quite rightly, that this does not preclude women, so why aren't there more women playing pinball? Perhaps it's because, for some people, pinball has a rather seedy, downbeat image and is therefore essentially "unfeminine." More important is the fact that many of the popular locations for pinball machines are bars. While it may be acceptable, socially, for men to enter such establishments unaccompanied, it's still not always that easy for a woman to do so, even today. Perhaps the reasons are physiological. One theory (among many others) is that in men the left side of the brain predominates and that this relates to coordination of the reflexes and reactions, while in women, the right side predominates, giving a greater affinity for color and design rather than activities that require hand/eye coordination. Such theories are not, of course, substantiated, and the general image of pinball, together with the location of the machines, are far more important factors in any explanation of male predominance in pinball playing.

The important thing to remember is that anyone can play pinball and, whatever its reputation, at 25 cents a game, it provides an inexpensive challenge to your reflexes and your tactical thinking under pressure.

BELOW Black Knight, *designed by Steve Ritchie, was the first game to use Magna-save.*

RIGHT Solar Fire *featured Magna-save and Multi-ball.*

Suddenly a terrifying explosion rips
through the sun and raging fires burn
out of control! The red hot solar
fires spawn a demonic breed of alien,
a breed never before known to man!

Your mission: To fight off
the alien menace and extinguish
the fires that feed their powers!

Height: 69½"; Depth: 53"
Width (cabinet): 22½"
Width (backbox): 30¼"
Weight: 290 lbs.
Instruction manual in game.

THE PINBALL COLLECTOR

Millions of people play the game in arcades, but a growing number of people enjoy the games in the comfort of their own homes, by installing a machine in the games room or den. There is also a growing élite of people who have more than one machine. The people I'm referring to are the collectors.

If you know where to look you can find collectors of everything from baseball cards to fire engines. So, why collect pinball machines? One thing's for sure — they're bigger than stamps! Very few people will be able to amass collections that run to double figures. So what's the attraction?

Well, unlike stamps, and many other collecting

LEFT *"Who dares to enter the tomb of the mighty Pharaoh?" Williams' advertising asked. Lighting up* PHARAOH *opened up the "hidden tomb" or "slave's tomb" for a free ball.*

BELOW *Another game with Magnasave,* Grand Lizard *utilized alphanumeric displays.*

Height: 73¾" (187 cm)
Height with backbox folded: 53" (135 cm)
Width: 30¼" (77 cm)
Depth: 53" (135 cm)
Weight: 225 lbs. (102 kg.) uncrated
        245 lbs. (111 kg.) crated
NOTICE: "GRAND LIZARD"
is a trademark of Williams Electronics Games, Inc.
© 1986, WILLIAMS ELECTRONICS GAMES, INC.

BELOW Firepower, *designed by Steve Richie, was a speaking pintable, a classic combination of Multi-ball and lane-change.*

RIGHT Eight Ball Champ *capitalized on the success of* Eight Ball deLuxe; *the main characters in the back glass bear an uncanny resemblance to two Bally game designers.*

Here's an exciting new game to rack up profits for you. Featuring great shots all over and player-controlled lights, this classic pinball-pool combination has never been more fun or more challenging.

MYLSTAR

hobbies, pinball machines offer not only the satisfaction of collecting but also the entertainment of playing and the challenge of active involvement with the technology. You can understand, maintain and repair the machine to a high standard of performance, and it's as satisfying as maintaining and tuning an automobile.

Collectors are attracted for various reasons: some appreciate the machines as relics of a bygone era, but call in an "expert" to tune and maintain them, just as they do with the family car. These "experts" may be collectors in their own right: people whose main thrill is derived from taking a piece of non-working equipment, either old technology (electro-mechanical) or "state of the art" (microprocessor controlled) and restoring it to its original working condition.

Another kind of person who is likely to be a collector is the "ultimate player." There is nothing casual about his play. He has wholeheartedly picked up the gauntlet thrown down by the industrial revolution, and is deeply engaged in the continuing war of man versus machine.

So far, we've heard about the collectors but what of their collections? These can have many different themes.

> There are collections based on:
>
> **ERAS** fifties, sixties, seventies, etc
> **MANUFACTURERS** Bally, Williams, Gottlieb, etc
> **TECHNOLOGIES** pre-electricity, electro-mechanical, electronic
> **GAME THEMES** card games, pool games, space themes, etc
> **STYLE OF GAMES** add-a-ball, replay, multiball, magna-save, etc
> **LIMITED PRODUCTION RUNS**

Of course it is possible to mix'n'match combinations, so you might find a collector who specializes in Gottlieb add-a-ball games of the sixties.

For those collectors who don't have the space, or perhaps the money, to collect the actual machines there is still the opportunity to collect "flyers" or other pinball ephemera.

Rack 'em Up *was one of the few Gottlieb games produced during the Mylstar era.*

BELOW Jive Time *featured a spinner on the back glass which was activated when the player trapped the ball in the saucer in the center of the playfield.*

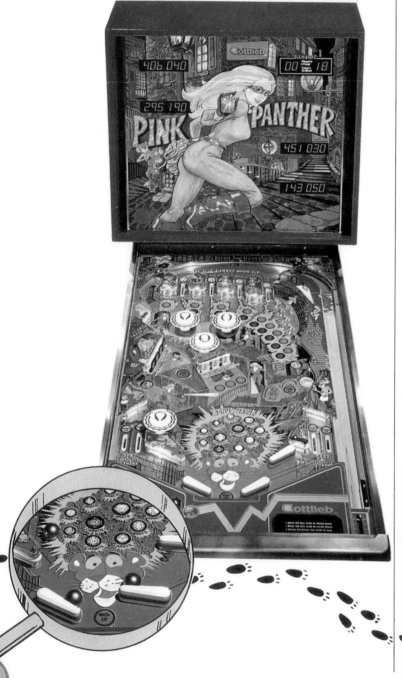

BELOW Pink Panther featured Multi-ball and encouraged the player to win specials by amassing diamonds.

BOTTOM RIGHT The Six Million Dollar Man is the only six-player electronic game produced to date.

THE CHALLENGE OF PINBALL

The challenge is man versus machine, in microcosm. It is taken up knowing that if you don't win, there are no serious consequences, just pure fun. The only price you pay for defeat is the cost of another game; another chance to beat the machine.

The beauty of it is that you don't have to wait months, weeks or even days for another crack at the title, you can start the next attack in minutes.

Emotionally, playing pinball offers a safe outlet for aggression, anger and frustration. Sensually, it offers physical involvement, stimulating the senses with color, lights and sounds. Cerebrally, there is the constant implementation of strategy, decision-making and review of gameplan.

As well as all this, playing pinball offers escape: for maximum results the player must give total commitment and concentration to the fantasy world of pinball with its themes of space travel, mythology, etc. But this commitment need only last 3-5 minutes, the average duration of a game. For this time the player can be oblivious to everything else, all that exists is the world of pinball held between his hands.

WHERE TO PLAY PINBALL

In the 1980s it is virtually impossible to watch a rock movie or video and not see a pinball machine. For example today I watched thirty minutes of television and saw two programs containing amusement machines. One was set in an amusement arcade and the other took place in a bar. In the movie *Superman IV*, the evil genius, Lex Luthor, has two pinball machines in his apartment.

The three most popular places for playing pinball are amusement arcades, bars and at home. Pinball machines have also been sighted in such diverse locations as airports, laundromats, restaurants pharmacies (Mexico); and markets in Fez, Morocco and Jerusalem. All these are in addition to the more usual locations of amusement arcades by the shore, fast food stores and shopping malls. So, though some people think pinball is obsolete, a relic of the past, in reality it is enjoying a post-video-game boom and is very much a part of the eighties with a bright future.

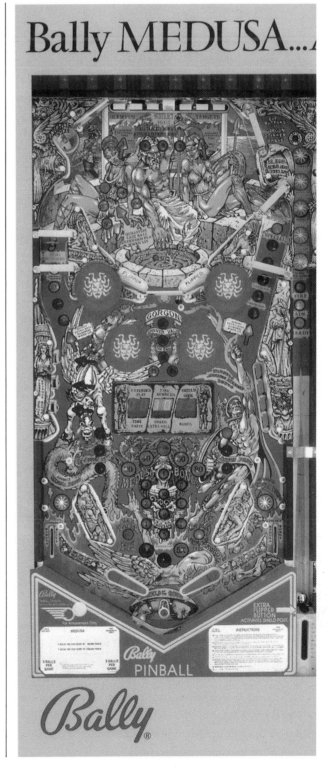

ABOVE *Detail of* Medusa *back glass.*
RIGHT *Medusa featured a "Shield of the Gods" post activated by a* separate button on the right-hand side of the cabinet; the post could send the ball back into play after it had passed behind the flippers.

- 2 SETS OF DROP TARGETS RIGHT IN THE FLIPPER FIRING LINE FOR TERRIFIC SHOOTING ACTION.
- HITTING ALL 4 GREEN DROP TARGETS LIGHTS EXTRA BALL FEATURE TARGET.
- BONUS VALUE DOUBLED BY KNOCKING DOWN 5 WHITE DROP TARGETS.
- MAKING 1 TO 5 NUMBERED SEQUENCE LIGHTS 2 ROLLOVERS FOR "SPECIALS" AND INCREASE WHITE DROP TARGET VALUE TO 3 BONUS ADVANCES.
- KICK-OUT HOLE SCORES 1,000 TO 5,000 CONTROLLED BY GREEN DROP TARGETS.

WHEN TO PLAY PINBALL

If you don't have a machine at home, the opportunities to play pinball are restricted, nevertheless . . .

. . . *Playing in the morning* is a good way to prepare for the day. Whereas breakfast may serve to fuel the body, pinball can enliven both mind and spirit; think of it as a limbering-up exercise.

. . . *Playing during the day,* eg during coffee and lunch breaks, is a good way of changing gear and relieving frustration, aggression, boredom or stress. If your daytime environment has a pinball machine or there is one nearby, you are fortunate.

. . . *Play pinball at the end of your working day!* Whether you work or study, playing pinball at this

time offers an excellent opportunity to get the day out out of your system. Alternatively, it can be the free-way that allows you to change the pace from daytime to evening. You may wish to use this opportunity to go from a frenetic day to a relaxed evening by having a combative game to get the last vestiges of aggression from your system. Alternatively, after a combative day you might choose to play a slower, more strategic game, carefully placing shots where they will be most advantageous. The options are manifold.

So early evening has passed. What now? Why not . . . *spend the evening at the pintable* in the company of friends, challenging each other for the high score of the evening. Or perhaps you'll want to focus your competitive instincts against the machine itself and continue the ongoing battle of man versus machine. Either way you can be sure the evening will produce a winner!

HOW TO PLAY PINBALL

To the uninitiated, pinball is a game of chance rather than a game of skill. But, to anyone who gives the subject a moment's intelligent thought, this is blatantly untrue. The movement of the steel ball around the playfield is subject to the laws of physics. The laws of physics are constant. Therefore pinball cannot be a game of chance. The player has, in addition, three ways of influencing the movement of the ball: the plunger, the flippers and nudging the machine. You need to master these basic skills if you want to play pinball consistently well. Additional features are built into the games from time to time. Mastery of these brings advanced skills. Such features may include:

"MAGNA-SAVE"

Black Knight (Williams 1980), *Solar Fire* (Williams 1981), *Jungle Lord* (Williams 1981), *Pharoah* (Williams 1981) and *Grand Lizard* (Williams 1986).

"LANE CHANGE"

Firepower (Williams 1980), *Eight Ball Champ* (Bally 1985), *Rack 'Em Up* (Gottlieb 1983).

"MULTIBALL"

Centaur (Bally 1981), *High Speed* (Williams 1985), *Flight 2000* (Stern 1980), *Monte Carlo* (Gottlieb 1986), *Pink Panther* (Gottlieb 1981).

"UP-POST"

Jive Time (Williams 1970), *Six Million Dollar Man* (Bally 1978).

OPPOSITE Vulcan *was a typical Gottlieb four-player game of the 1970s.*

ABOVE Centaur, *designed by Jim Patla, was inspired by the 1950s Bally game Balls-a-Popping, but the art, with its black and white graphics, was pure video game.*

The Plunger   This is the mechanism for sending the ball into play. Its use is both critical and skillful. On better games skillful use of the plunger will enable the player to score more points or replay. By careful timing of the release of the ball from the shooter lane, which is controlled by the plunger, there is an opportunity, for example, to increase the value of the Gorgon spinner on *Medusa* (Bally 1981). On *Space Shuttle* (Williams 1984) the force with which the plunger is released determines through which of the U, S or A lanes the ball enters the playfield. Completing

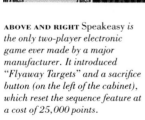

ABOVE AND RIGHT Speakeasy *is the only two-player electronic game ever made by a major manufacturer. It introduced "Flyaway Targets" and a sacrifice button (on the left of the cabinet), which reset the sequence feature at a cost of 25,000 points.*

"U.S.A." increases the value of the bonus multiplier. There is further opportunity to score through the necessary lane(s) by skillful use of the "lane change" button. This rearranges the "lit" lane(s) so that the ball enters through an unlit lane, giving a better chance of increasing the bonus multiplier.

Another possible arrangement is for the ball to enter the playfield via a "rollover" lane with a card or letter value, where completing the sequence lights S P E C I A L , *Vulcan* (Gottlieb 1977), *Speakeasy* (Bally 1982), *Oxo* (Williams 1974), share this feature. Here the skilled player will be using the plunger to ensure the ball enters via any rollover lanes required to complete the sequence.

Nudging (also known as "Graunching" or "Using Body English," often shortened to "English"). This is the most contentious of the basic skills. Those who do not possess it often see it as cheating, but there is a subtle skill in nudging the machine to keep the ball in play or, by gently rolling it against a bumper skirt, causing a spurt of action that breathes life into a slow-moving ball. It is simply the pinball equivalent of the athlete anticipating the starting pistol or the long jumper judging the take-off position in order not to overstep the mark. Besides, the pintable itself anticipates nudging. Inside the game are several switches designed to detect excessive English. The sensitivity of these switches can be adjusted to allow greater or less tolerance. In pinball, the machine is always the final arbiter.

The penalty for overstepping the mark is *"TILT,"* which can attract one of several penalties. In "Sudden Death," the rest of the game is forfeit; alternatively all cumulative features may be reset to minimum value and ball in play is forfeit; or the ball in play may be forfeit, along with any bonus earned. There is an interesting variation in the case of "add-a-ball" games such as *Square Head* (Gottlieb 1963) where the penalty is usually loss of ball in play plus the next ball.

The Flippers Their skillful use involves three aims. First, stopping the ball draining from the bottom of the playfield and going out of play. Second, the flippers are used to control the speed of the ball. By catching it on the flipper, you can slow its movement. Alternatively, the flippers can be used to speed up the movement of the ball by propelling it up the downward slope of the playfield. Third – and this is what sorts out the skilled player from the casual interloper – the flippers are used to direct the ball to strategic parts of the playfield where it can be of most benefit in scoring points, replays or extra balls.

Flippers are ultimately the power behind the ball.

■ *KNOW THE GAME* To get the most pleasure from a game it is important to know it well. This will tell you how to get the most points and what has to be done to earn replays. Often games have a bias. That is to say, the best strategy for getting the most play for your money may be to play for replays (i.e. "Specials") rather than a high score.

There are three ways to find out about the game. You can read the "game card", usually to be found on the bottom left hand corner of the playfield. Sometimes, however, the card may be missing, or does not correspond accurately to the game settings. As games get more complex it is difficult to describe all the game features on the card. *Centaur* offers the player help to understand the game in a highly innovative way: . . . if the player presses either of the flipper buttons before starting the game, the machine will speak the instructions while lighting up the corresponding features on the playfield.

Another way of learning the game is by observing other players; but most pinball enthusiasts prefer learning by doing. The personal challenge is after all the whole joy of pinball, and discovering the idiosyncracies of each machine for yourself is probably more satisfying.

So put in your quarter and see what charms the game has to tempt you!

THE EARLY DAYS
(1930–44)

*T*o most players, pinball is a combination of well-timed flipper shots, frenzied ball action, flashing lights and pleasing sounds. The first pinball machines had none of these features, and were very different from what most people think of as pinball today.

Pinball traces its roots to bagatelle, a game in which marbles are shot onto a playing area dotted with pockets assigned various point values. After all of the marbles are shot, the player adds up the scores of the pockets into which the marbles have rolled. Although bagatelle games became a popular parlor recreation for the wealthy in the late 19th century, the first coin-operated bagatelle-styled machines began appearing in the late 1920s. Most of these small countertop devices were handmade, and played primarily in male-oriented locations such as saloons and barbershops. Bagatelle manufacturers were scattered across the country, but most were based in Chicago. With its central location and the ready availability of manufacturing tools and equipment, Chicago quickly established itself as the pinball capital of the world, a distinction which the city still holds today.

In 1930, a young businessman named David Gottlieb bought the manufacturing rights to *Bingo*, a coin-operated bagatelle game made by a company called The Bingo Novelty Company. The game was a limited success, but inspired Gottlieb to create a machine of his own, and later that year, he introduced *Baffle Ball*. Gottlieb had been producing coin-operated games for several years (his coin-op grip testing machines of the twenties were very popular), but it was *Baffle Ball* which established D. Gottlieb & Co. as the world's first successful pinball manufacturer. More than 50,000 *Baffle Balls* were sold in 1931 for $17.50 apiece. Even during the depths of the Depression, players dropped their pennies into *Baffle Ball* (which gave seven balls for one cent). At about 16 by 24 inches, *Baffle Ball* was typical of most pinball games being sold at this time. Although

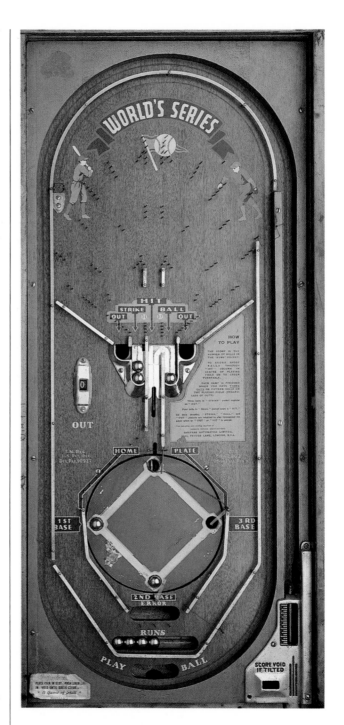

ABOVE *On early games, such as* World Series, *the ball would travel a full circuit of the perimeter before scoring!*

ABOVE *Pinball didn't take long to cross the Atlantic; this was a British trade show in 1935.*

LEFT *The precursor of pinball, a 1920s bagatelle game.*

an optional stand was available, *Baffle Ball* was designed as a countertop game. It had five high-scoring holes in the center of the playfield; if the balls missed these holes, they would roll down to the row of lower-scoring pockets at the bottom of the game. The scoring holes were actually small pockets surrounded by a ring of nails or pins, which is how pinball got its name. *Baffle Ball* had no flippers or electricity, and the only sounds were those made by the small steel marbles hitting the nails.

In 1931, Raymond Maloney, one of Gottlieb's distributors, formed the Lion Manufacturing Company to produce his own pinball called *Ballyhoo*, named after a popular magazine. *Ballyhoo* was just as successful as *Baffle Ball*, and Maloney soon changed the

21

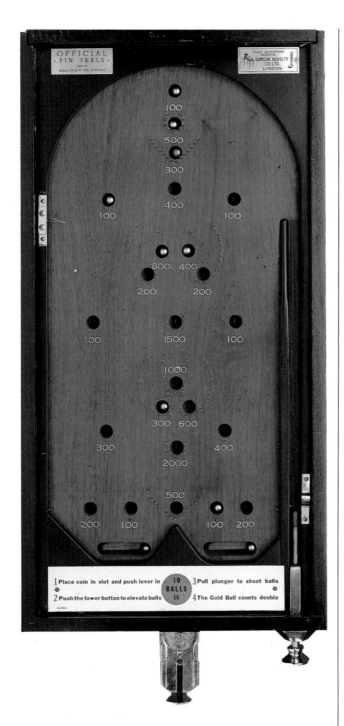

Mills' Official, *a countertop game released in 1932.*

TOP RIGHT Diamond-Flash, *another countertop game from the 1930s; mid-way through the decade, countertops were disappearing in favor of larger machines with legs.*

name of his company to Bally to reflect the game's popularity. *Ballyhoo*, at $16.00, was priced lower than *Baffle Ball*, and was even available with a nickel chute, a testimony to pinball's success.

Baffle Ball and *Ballyhoo* together sold more than 100,000 games, and it wasn't long before other pinball manufacturers began entering the field. Chicago Coin, formed by Sam Wolberg and Sam Gensbert in 1931 as a distributor, was one of the many manufacturers to produce pingames, and survived for more than four decades. Other early pinball manufacturers that met with success in the 1930s (and beyond) included Daval, Stoner, Keeney, Exhibit and Genco. More than 150 companies claimed to be pinball manufacturers at this time! Most of these were tiny one- or two-man operations which produced handmade machines in a garage or basement to meet the tremendous demand for the games. Most disappeared without a trace, although by a twist of fate, any one of them could have stumbled upon a winning game and established themselves as a major manufacturer.

By 1933, manufacturers had become more innovative in an attempt to set themselves apart from their competitors. Rock-Ola, a company that found tremendous success with jukeboxes, produced several games in this era, including *World's Fair Jig Saw* (1933), commemorating the fair's 1933 Chicago presentation. *World's Fair Jig Saw* featured a hidden puzzle in the center of the playfield; landing the balls in the proper holes would flip over selected pieces of the puzzle, with the ultimate reward of revealing the entire puzzle awaiting skilled players. *World's Fair Jig Saw* was typical of many 1933 machines which placed increasing emphasis on artwork. Earlier games

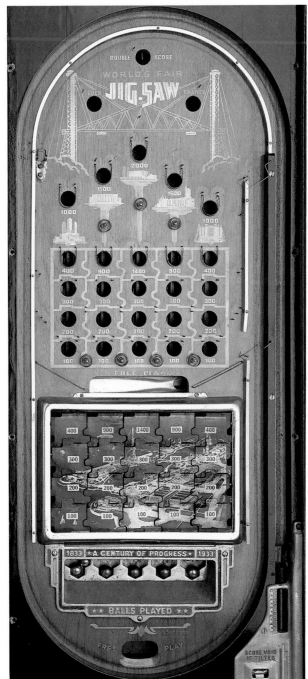

LEFT Goofy *was the second game made by Bally, distributed in August 1932.*

ABOVE Jigsaw *was made by the Rock-Ola Manufacturing Corporation, celebrating the 1933 World's Fair held in San Francisco.*

had little artistic design; many, like *Ballyhoo*, were extremely colorful, although artwork was limited limited primarily to eye-catching shapes and patterns. However, *World's Fair Jig Saw* and other games offered players something exciting to look at. New pinball themes were being explored, and the artwork on many games was becoming very detailed.

Another leap forward in pinball's evolution was unveiled in 1933 on *Contact*. Designed for Pacific Amusement Manufacturing by Harry Williams (who was responsible for many important pinball inventions before forming Williams Electronics in the 1940s), *Contact* was the first battery-operated pinball machine. If the ball landed in a special hole on the playfield, an electrically operated solenoid kicker would eject the ball, while at the same time ringing a bell (making *Contact* the first game featuring sound). Mills' *Canon Fire* (1934) was another battery-operated pin-game (which used six batteries) and

ABOVE *The object of Jigsaw was to complete the puzzle; scores would be totaled by counting the value of the exposed pieces. A winning score would be rewarded by the person behind the counter. The payout would vary, just as the price of playing the game varied,* *according to the location: 1c here, 5c round the corner in a classier joint.*
OPPOSITE *Mills' Tycoon, distributed in August 1936, was a gambling game which allowed up to seven players to bet on the outcome.*

TYCOON

DESCRIBED BY 1000 OPERATORS AS THE GREATEST COIN MACHINE EVER BUILT

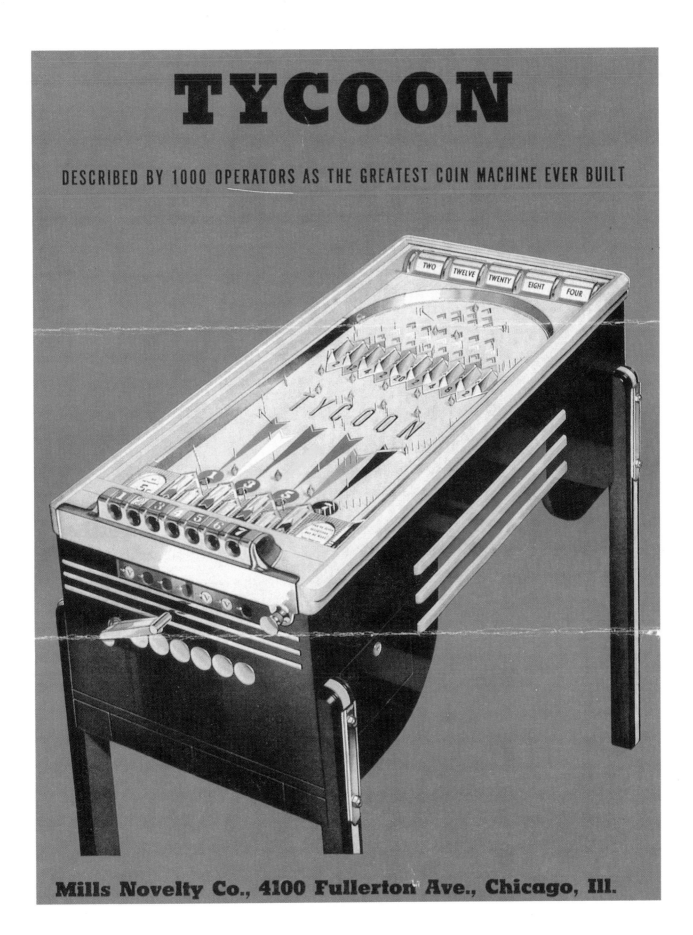

Mills Novelty Co., 4100 Fullerton Ave., Chicago, Ill.

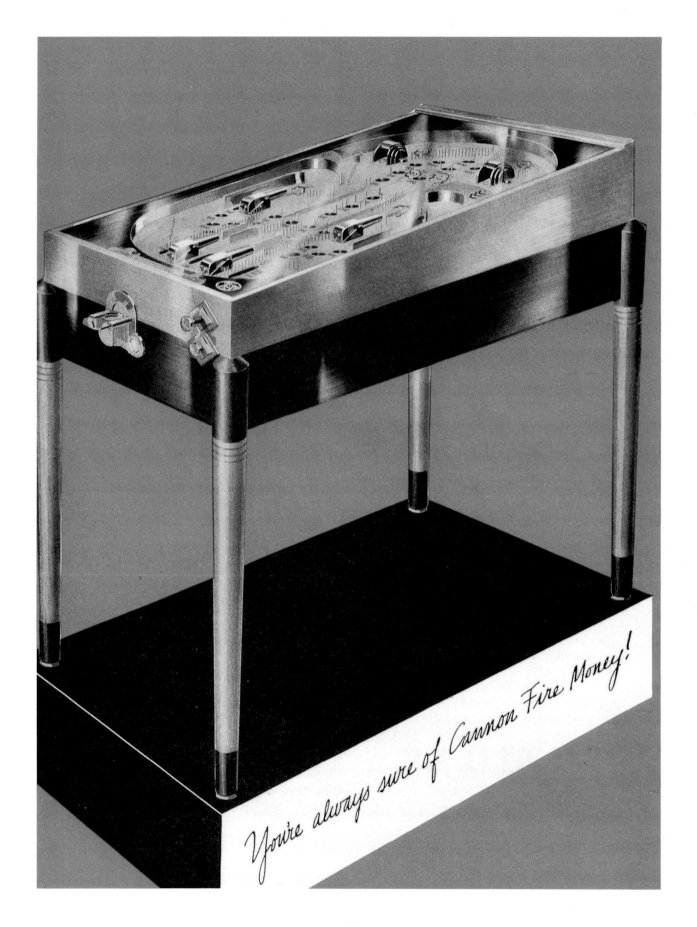

You're always sure of Cannon Fire Money!

featured four solenoid-powered cannons that shot the balls around the playfield. Mills' promotional material stated:

"Cannon Fire has variety of action – over 124,000 separate and distinct shots! Its simplified mechanism assures trouble free performance. It's a big table (48 inches long and 26 inches wide), beautiful, modern – locations won't let you move it! Let Cannon Fire be your basic money-maker – measure its life in YEARS *instead of weeks!"*

Exhibit's *Rebound* (1934) was another battery-operated game "with thrilling double deck action," according to the company. *Rebound* had an electrical kicker which rocketed the ball through a wire ramp over the center of the playfield for added ball action. This new electrical technology was costly, though; most games now sold for about $35.00 to $40.00.

Transformers were added to pinball in 1935, allowing the games to be plugged into standard electrical outlets. Solenoid action was included in nearly every machine by this time, with shooting balls and ringing bells now commonplace. A few manufacturers were still producing battery-operated games, though. One company, Evans, even produced an all-mechanical game called *Kings Of The Turf* in 1935, and claimed that its pinball was more reliable than battery-operated machines.

Electricity presented new pinball strategies to players, who could now be directed to aim for specific high-scoring targets by lights. "Lights out" action was popular on games because the machines could "react" to the player's scoring. By the end of the decade, "lights out" had become pinball's most popular scoring strategy. Genco's *Bang* (1939) was typical when it advertised new "skill-thrill holes" that "put out four-lights-at-a-time . . . so the player can put out all 12 lights and get a winner with only 3 balls. What an irresistible come-on!!"

Pinball's format was undergoing other changes at this time. Since the days of tabletop bagatelles, most machines had used small steel marble-sized balls (although some pinballs were closer to the size of ball

FAR LEFT *Mills'* Cannon Fire *was released in July 1934. The game was 48in long and 26in wide – the company made a big thing out of the enormous size. It usually cost 5c a shot.*

LEFT *Jennings'* Sportsman *(left) and* Wall street *(right); these are actually one-arm bandits disguised as pintables! (Note the arm on the right.)*

LEFT *Genco's* Subway, *released in September 1934. Genco was set up by the enterprising Genberg brothers.*

RIGHT *Compare the complexity of the 1950s* Jigsaw *from Williams with the original* Jigsaw *on page 24; on the later machine, a mirrored back glass would gradually reveal the image as the score increased.*

bearings). These balls were perfectly suited to early pinball machines; the electrical solenoid power of most '30s games was weak by today's standards, but it was sufficient to propel these tiny pinballs around the playfield. When the machines began getting larger later in the decade, marble-sized pinballs were phased out in favor of the larger balls found on today's games. By the late 1930s, all of the elaborate kicking devices which had rocketed tiny balls upwards across the playfield had disappeared and the play action became vertical, with the balls simply scoring points as they rolled down the field.

But a lot of pinball's appeal had worn off by the mid thirties and only a handful of manufacturers remained. Some people believed that pinball was just a passing fad whose time had come and gone. In an effort to attract players back to the games, new concepts were introduced.

Pinball manufacturers tried broadening the games' appeal by producing one-ball payout machines. These pinballs rewarded the player with cash payouts for high scores. Most one-ball pinball machines could accept several coins per game, which increased the size of the payout. Mills' *Tycoon* was a typical one-ball payout pinball. According to the company's 1936 promotional material:

"Mills' Tycoon, the Tycoon of all pin tables, is thundering its mighty way up and down the country, making all other tables look weak by comparison."

Tycoon had seven payout pockets at the bottom of the playfield; the player would "bet" on the pocket into which he thought the ball would roll by inserting his nickel into one of the seven coin chutes. Of course, players could hedge their bets by depositing nickels into all seven coin chutes, but if the ball hit certain targets in the center of the playfield before dropping into the payout pocket, the payout would be even higher.

"Tycoon not only has suspense, it is noted for its challenge to individual skill, for the player can definitely aim, by means of his single shot, at raising the amount of reward which will be his if the ball lands in the hole he selects." Payout games badly tarnished pinball's image in several areas. Many cities and states equated all pinballs with slot machines, and banned the games as gambling devices. Most of the pinball machines being played at this time were for amusement only, built without any means of paying out, although many lawmakers and elected officials couldn't differentiate between the games, resulting in all pinballs — amusement and payout — being banned. This gambling stigma still haunts pinball in some areas even today.

Some payout games dispensed tickets rather than coins. Most of these were manufacturered between 1934 and 1938 as an alternative to cash payouts. High-scoring players could trade these tickets in for additional games on the machine, prizes or even money, although ticket dispensing pinballs were never as popular with players as cash payouts.

While payout games were stirring up trouble in some areas, another reward system for players was also developed at about the same time. Until about 1935, pinball machines couldn't reward skillful players with anything except the enjoyment of the game,

although some locations offered weekly prizes (such as a pack of cigarettes) to the highest-scoring player of the week. But starting with Rock-Ola's *Flash* in 1935, pinballs began awarding replays – free games –to players. These replays could be awarded both for high scores and for landing the ball in a "free play" hole. Another 1935 Rock-Ola pingame, *Gold Rush*, was a combination replay/payout machine. As on most replay games, *Gold Rush's* free play holes were strategically located under playfield obstacles where balls would be unlikely to roll very often. However,

Gold Rush was also a one-ball payout machine which gave players the chance to win something even better than replays – cash. Replay pinballs were more readily accepted in most areas than payout machines, although some lawmakers considered even a free game as "a thing of value" and outlawed these games as gambling devices. Some pinballs were produced in two models – novelty (for amusement only) and free play, although most replay machines featured different names and playfield layouts than novelty games, to help operators distinguish between the two.

In 1934, Harry Williams (designer of *Contact*) invented one of the most infamous pinball devices – the tilt mechanism. Until that time, there was no dependable way of preventing players from lifting and shaking the machines to achieve high scores. In fact, the lightweight countertop games almost encouraged cheating, and operators found many ingenious ways to prevent players from abusing machines. Weighing down the games with sandbags was one method, while another (more painful) approach was to have several sharp nails hanging out underneath the game to prevent players from banging on the bottom of the cabinet.

Bally's *Signal* (1934) was the first pinball to include Williams' anti-cheating device, originally called a stool pigeon. A small steel ball rested atop a one-inch pedestal, and if the machine was jostled, the ball would fall off the pedestal and land on a metal ring, completing an electrical circuit and ending the game. Williams renamed his anti-cheating device the "tilt" after he overheard some players using the term. Today, the word "tilt" has become a part of the English language. Early tilt mechanisms were visible to the player, and even included a tiny arrow which normally pointed to "OK" but would move to "Tilt" if the player activated the device. In 1935, Williams invented the pendulum tilt. A chain would hang in the center of a metal ring; if the chain made contact with the ring because of excessive shaking, the game would end. Today's pinballs use an almost-identical tilt device, with a cone-shape plumb bob replacing the chain.

Pinball machines had grown larger in the mid thirties, after manufacturers began attaching legs to the games, moving away from countertop pins. At about the same time, small backboxes also began

LEFT *Chicago Coin Machine's* Topper, *released in April 1936.*

OPPOSITE *"Loop-the loop! Double deck thrills! Action – action – action!" The Exhibit Supply Company's* Rebound.

REBOUND

by EXHIBIT

ONCE more—EXHIBIT presents a marvelous—money maker—as usual— that is far beyond the ordinary animated pin game of today.

AGAIN—we give you a game with new dazzling plays to thrill players—combined with more money making features ever built into one game—to keep the PROFIT making pot boiling for you.

In "REBOUND"—you will see a spectacular performance with new LIVE amazing action,—with balls—actually looping the loop—rolling on double deck with sky ride thrills—and balls rebounding—rebounding— and rebounding with machine gun action.

It's a combination skill and pleasure game with no lost balls—built purposely to attract amateur and skill shooters.

REBOUND

has already proven itself a smashing sensation on the West Coast, and is now manufactured under exclusive license from the California Games Co. of Los Angeles—

Now built in a popular location size—19x38 inches—with the usual EXHIBIT precision and quality.

WITH THRILLING DOUBLE DECK ACTION

31

to appear on the games, and some manufacturers used this area for automatic scorekeeping. Bally's *Rockelite* was the first game to include automatic scoring on the backglass. A series of numbers, in increasing increments, was drawn on the backglass, which was illuminated by small light bulbs behind the glass to keep track of the player's score. As backglasses grew larger by the end of the 1930s, more artwork was added. Manufacturers started taking advantage of this extra space by adding animation. Moving figures would jump around in the backbox attracting attention (and repeat play) when players hit certain targets. Harry Hoppe Corp.'s *Taps*, for example, featured a black minstrel man character which would perform a short dance.

Pinball animation was often coordinated with game play. Bally's *Fifth Inning* (1939) was a baseball-theme machine which featured tiny metal men circling a baseball diamond in the backbox; playfield features scored singles, doubles, triples and home runs to advance the "ballplayers" and score runs. *Fifth Inning* sold for $79.50 and was typical of the way animation was used to attract players. Backbox animation remained popular through the 1970s.

One of the most important pinball developments of the 1930s premiered on Bally's *Bumper* (1936). Until *Bumper*, scoring was determined entirely by the pocket into which the ball had dropped. *Bumper* introduced bumpers – metal posts surrounded by coiled springs. When the ball touched these posts, points were scored. Bumpers wouldn't have been practical even a few years earlier before electricity made automatic scoring possible. Bumpers quickly became the most popular playfield scoring device, and many games (such as Bally's 1937 *Airway*) had nothing but an array of bumpers on the playfield.

Players' fascination with bumpers continued through the early 1940s. Chicago Coin's *Buckaroo* (1939) had 15 bumpers – five red, five yellow and five green – which lit at various scores to award replays. Gottlieb's *Bowling Alley* (1940) had ten bumpers (corresponding

to bowling pins) which would award free games when all ten bumpers had been hit. Very few games of this era had less than ten bumpers, while most had many more. Stoner's *Ali Baba* pinball (1940) may hold the record with a whopping 24 bumpers! These early

OPPOSITE *The Harry Hoppe Corporation's* Taps, *released in May 1939, featured in animated back glass and "modernist" design.*

BELOW *As a follow-up to their* Airway *of 1933, Bally produced a much-revised* Airway *in 1937, including a "progressive score skill objective feature" and illuminated double-action bumpers.*

33

pinball bumpers had no solenoid kicker action and could only score points, they were always central to the games' strategy. Daval's *High-Lite* (1939) was one of many games to feature lighted bumpers. *High-Lite* was:

"*A combination Hi-Score and Lights-Out Masterpiece with Intermediate Awards! Combines the* TWO *greatest player-appeal principles ever known –* HI-SCORE PLAY *with adjustable shifting lights and intermediate awards galore . . . plus the new* LIGHTS-OUT ACTION *with mounting awards after all lit-up bumpers are put out! What a combination! . . . and what a game!*"

Manufacturers could create only a limited number of playfield arrangements using the few pinball features available at this time, so other innovations began appearing. Gottlieb's 1939 *Lot-O-Smoke* pinball was identical to the company's *Lot-O-Fun* (1939), except that *Lot-O-Smoke* featured pictures of several popular brands of cigarettes on the backglass to

CHAMP
FIRST!
WITH REVOLUTIONARY
NEW HIT-FEATURES!

NEW "BIG WINNER" APPEAL!
Because player builds up amazing award total, while playing game!

NEW PERFECT INVISIBLE
PERCENTAGE CONTROL!
First time ever on Novelty or Free Play game!

NEW LIVE BALL
ACTION—
Alternate type bumpers, Free Ball return and other sensational features!

NOVELTY
$89.50

FREE PLAY
$99.50

IMMEDIATE DELIVERY

ABOVE Batting Champ, *released by Gottlieb in July of 1939; Gottlieb had survived the decade.*

appeal to pinball's young, mostly male players.

Some gimmick features were also appearing on games, such as the "jinx eliminator" on Bally's *Pick-Em* (1939), a game with 12 numbered bumpers. The object was to hit all 12 bumpers, and Bally's new feature let players select one "free" bumper which wouldn't need to be hit. "Every player has his 'hoo-doo' number which he considers extra hard to hit . . . and *Pick Em* permits the player to dodge the jinx before he shoots! He simply turns the Self-Spotter Dial (on the front of the machine) and 'spots' his own number," according to Bally. Gottlieb used a similar device on its 1940 *Lite-O-Card*, which included 13 bumpers; the player selected one of four bingo-style cards on the backglass and then tried to hit the lit bumpers to complete horizontal, vertical or lines on the cards.

Pinball had lost much of its luster by the end of the decade; when the Depression ended and prosperity returned, the vicarious thrills of manipulating steel balls around a colorful playfield no longer appealed to many players. Although pinball had gone through a gradual (though startling) evolution in only ten short years, the games were becoming predictable; every machine had a similar arrangement of bumpers and rollovers with only slight variations. While pinball games of every era are sought by collectors, the machines of the late 1930s and early 1940s seem to generate the least amount of interest among today's collectors.

In 1942, as the U.S. economy began gearing up for World War Two, pinball production stopped. All of the manufacturers' production lines shifted from pinball to wartime products. Gottlieb, Bally, Genco, Exhibit, Keeney and others converted their assembly lines to produce such things as machine gun parts, rocket components and parachute equipment.

To satisfy the demand for new pinball machines, pinball conversions began appearing. Although complete new games couldn't be produced because of the war, several small companies started offering kits to convert existing machines into "new" games. A new backglass (with a different name and artwork) was supplied, along with new plastic playfield covers to give the appearance of an all-new machine. Many of these conversions had wartime themes, such as *Smack The Japs* (1943) by Victory Games, *Victorious 1944* (1944) by Westerhaus and *Invasion* (1943), also by Westerhaus. War-theme pinball had been around since the mid 1930s; one of these was Rock-Ola's 1935 *Bomber*, which "fits in perfectly right now with all the news of war and bombings in the papers," according to the company. Most of these wartime conversion kit manufacturers disappeared without a trace even before the war ended.

The war temporarily halted pinball production, but by the end of 1945, the US was returning to a normal economy. All of the major manufacturers put pinball games back on the assembly line, and once again, pinball was back in the spotlight.

THE POST-WAR ERA
(1945-60)

After the end of World War Two, pinball manufacturers returned to production with new games celebrating America's victory. Post-war machines such as Gottlieb's *Stage Door Canteen* (1946) and Bally's *Victory Special* (1946) appealed to players as much as *Smack The Japs* had only a few years earlier.

Because pinball companies had been forced to put new game designs on "hold" during the war, most post-war pinballs resembled those that had been produced earlier in the decade, and included arrays of bumpers and rollover lanes. Most of these machines featured numbered bumpers; players tried to hit all of the bumpers (or a combination of bumpers and rollovers) for a replay. A newly developed playfield feature was the "kickout saucer," a small pocket (often in the center of the playfield) which briefly caught the ball before a solenoid-activated kicker ejected it back into play.

Following the war, two new pinball manufacturers sprang up. Williams Manufacturing was created by designer/inventor Harry Williams in 1946; its first game, which went into production on February 1, was *Suspense*. Another pinball pioneer of the thirties, Lyn Durant, formed United Manufacturing at about the same time, joining Bally, Gottlieb, Exhibit, Genco, Keeney and Chicago Coin in the pinball field.

Pinball machines were enjoying moderate (though not spectacular) popularity in the late forties when an accidental invention took players by storm and changed the game forever.

A Gottlieb engineer named Harry Mabs had been working on a baseball-style pitch-and-bat game in 1947. These pitch-and-bat games were similar in appearance to pinballs, but had a row of targets at the top of the playfield rather than bumpers and rollovers. When the player pressed a button on the front of the cabinet, a tiny ball would pop out from the center of the playfield. The player then pressed another control button which operated a bat at the bottom of the game, to hit the ball back up the playfield at the targets. As in baseball, the player had only once chance to hit each ball after it was released, so he had to time the swing of the bat carefully. As the story goes, Mabs accidentally activated the bat several times in succession (bypassing the machine's built-in delay system which normally prevented the bat from swinging more than once after each ball was released). Mabs applied this continuous bat action to pinball, and added several player-controlled bats to hit the ball up the playfield. Mabs' next pinball machine, *Humpty Dumpty*, appeared in the fall of 1947 with a new invention – flippers.

LEFT *Three games from the fifties, with the almost universal wooden rails of the decade; all three were produced by Gottlieb, where designer Ray Parker was producing some of the most attractive pinball art ever.*

OPPOSITE *Detail from* Lady Robin Hood *back glass, released by Gottlieb in January 1948.*

Humpty Dumpty sported three pairs of these two-inch "flipper bumpers," as they were originally called. Two flippers were placed near the bottom of the playfield, two in the middle and two at the top, so players could relay the ball up the entire playfield. For the first time, players could actively manipulate the ball, rather than watch passively as it simply rolled down. Promotional material declared *Humpty Dumpty The greatest triumph in pin game history! Phenomenal is the word for this play-inspiring Gottlieb*

innovation! Unique flipper bumpers are motivated by sensitive finger-tip control buttons on each side of the cabinet. With skill and timing, player can control balls and send them zooming right back to the top of the playing field for additional scoring! The combination of controlled Flipper Bumper action and controlled ball action provides amazing earning power . . . a proven shot-in-the-arm for any location.

Within hours after *Humpty Dumpty's* unveiling at the Coin Machine Industries' annual trade show,

pinballs without flippers became obsolete. By the end of 1947, every pinball manufacturer had either produced its own flipper-equipped pinballs or had them under development. Players unanimously preferred the new machines, which were called flipper games to distinguish them from the one-ball payout "flipperless" games which were still in production. Before long, flipper-retrofit kits were being sold to add flipper action to older machines.

Flippers opened up new avenues in pinball design. Under the direction of head designer Harvey Heiss, Genco had some highly unusual playfields. *Rip Snorter* (1949) had seven kickout saucers in a verti-cal line across the center of the playfield, with a set of flippers at the lower left and right of the game, while *South Pacific* (1949) featured a diagonal row of ten kickout saucers.

Flippers were positioned differently on these early games from today's standard setups. Early flippers were arranged with the tips pointed toward the outside edges of the playfield rather than the center. Although this action was somewhat awkward by today's standards, players then were thrilled to have any flipper action at all. It wasn't until the early fifties that flippers were reversed into the same position that they are in today.

OPPOSITE *Genco's* Floating Power, *released December 1948.*

BELOW *Advertisement for Gottlieb's* Humpty Dumpty *(1947); the first game with flippers. Three flippers on the right, three on the left, and in comparison with today's standard layout, they're all "back-to-front!"*

RIGHT *The Four Horseman from Gottlieb (September 1950).*

Because of limitations in electrical current, the flipper games of the late 1940s had flippers that were very weak in comparison to later games. These machines usually required six flippers to maneuver the ball all the way up the playfield. Genco designer Steven Kordek engineered more powerful flippers on his company's games in the late forties and created the first pinball machine with only two flippers. Stronger flippers became standard on all manufacturers' games by the early fifties.

But popular as flipper pinballs had become, the market was saturated by 1950. With all the flipper games produced in 1948 and 1949 (plus all the flipper-retrofit kits), the demand for new pinball games had been pretty well filled. Chicago Coin, Exhibit, Keeney, Genco and Bally, all major pinball manufacturers since the thirties withdrew from pinball production to concentrate on building other arcade games. Only Gottlieb and Williams remained in constant pinball production through the 1950s.

ABOVE *Gottlieb's* Criss Cross *(February 1958); the fallen skier in the back glass is rumored to be David Gottlieb, the boss.*
BELOW LEFT Happy Days *from Gottlieb (July 1952), an example of the tic-tac-toe theme which has* been used by different designers right down to the present day (see page 101).

OPPOSITE Williams' *Spark Plugs; the object was to move the horses in the pack to the finishing line.*

Gottlieb quickly established itself as the "king" of pinball in the fifties. Although designer Harry Mabs had moved to Williams early in the decade (a move which he later said he regretted), Gottlieb pinball designer Wayne Neyens was responsible for most of the games which maintained the company's popularity throughout the decade, while over at Williams, designer Gordon Horlock (along with Mabs) was creating innovative playfields of his own.

Backbox animation was a steady attraction during the 1950s. Gottlieb in particular produced many innovative animated games, such as *Mermaid* (1951), which featured a 3-D "fisherman" in the backbox which would pull in a prize catch during high-scoring games. Williams used backbox animation as an integral part of the game. *Spark Plugs* (1951) was one of several of Williams' horse race games with moving thoroughbreds keyed into the game play. The six animated horses in the backbox were advanced by hitting the targets and bumpers, and if the player's randomly selected horse reached the finishing line

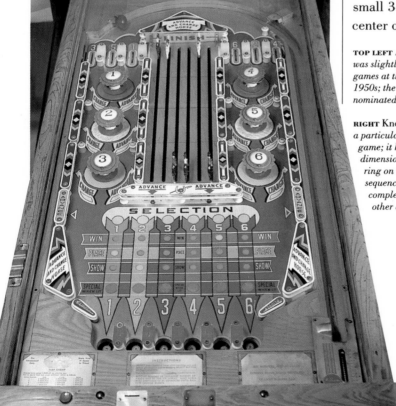

before the others, the player would receive a replay. Williams' *Sea Jockeys* (1951) had a similar strategy, but used speedboats instead of horses.

Backbox action was also used in other ways. Gottlieb's *Happy Days* (1952) had a tic-tac-toe motif, with large Xs and Os lighting in a grid in the backglass. *Happy Days* was one of the first machines to include "gobble holes" – drop-through scoring holes in the center of the playfield. Losing a ball in a gobble hole scored big points or replays, but also ended that ball – it was a tradeoff feature. *Happy Days* had *nine* gobble holes, but no outlanes or gap between the flippers. Each gobble hole would light a square of the backglass's tic-tac-toe board: three Xs or Os in a row awarded a replay.

Playfield animation also appeared on several games during the fifties. One of the most popular of these was Gottlieb's *Knockout* (1950), which featured two small 3-D "manikins" in a square boxing ring in the center of the playfield; hitting bumpers and rollovers

TOP LEFT AND LEFT Turf Champ *was slightly larger than most games at the beginning of the 1950s; the objective was to get your nominated horse first past the post.*

RIGHT Knockout *from Gottlieb was a particularly attractive animated game; it had tinplate three-dimensional figures in a boxing ring on the playfield; when the sequence was successfully completed, one would knock the other down.*

started the match. Gottlieb's *Wild West* (1951) included an "animated" Indian-head that dropped under the playfield when the target in front of it was hit. *Turf Champ* (1958) was another of Williams' horse race games, but unlike *Spark Plugs, Turf Champ* had the horses in the center of the playfield, separated from the ball action. Each of the six horses was on an individual vertical track, and started at the bottom of the playfield. Before the game, the player would pick one of the horses using a selector button on the front of the game, and all the horses would move ahead slowly, at different speeds, as playfield targets and bumpers were hit. The player could win a replay if his horse finished first, second or third, although *Turf Champ* had no scoring other than the horse-racing movement.

In 1951, the federal government passed a strict anti-gambling law which put an end to the one-ball and payout pinballs that had flourished since the thirties, but a new type of game was developed to fill the void. "Bingo" pinballs appeared in 1951, and were met with the same anti-gambling sentiments as one-ball pinballs. Most bingo games had 25 numbered trap holes on the playfield, and one or more bingo-style cards on the backglass. Before the start of the game, players could insert one coin or several to increase the odds of winning, then shoot five balls and try to light winning combinations on the bingo cards. Although bingo machines resembled flipper games at first glance, they played more like pre-flipper pinballs, with the plunger being the only player-operated control device on the machine. Bingo games could award only replays (rather than cash payouts), but lawmakers viewed them as gambling devices because the machines could register far more free plays than anyone could be expected to play — up to 999 replays. Very often, players would accumulate credits on bingo games and then be paid off in cash by the location owner, who would then knock credits off through a "hidden" button on the game. Today, bingo machines can be legally operated only in

ABOVE Jigsaw, *released in November of 1957, is a fairly rare machine. (The playfield is illustrated on page 29)*

BELOW *Gottlieb's* Bank-A-Ball *(1950) was based upon the ever-popular theme of pool.*

LEFT Gottlieb's replay game *Queen of Hearts* was released in 1952, with a handsome and detailed backglass.

BELOW *The goal in* Coronation *was to get four balls in a row on the vee configuration.*

RIGHT *Scantily clad women were almost a specialty of Gottlieb.*

BELOW RIGHT *"Tilt" on Gottlieb's* Daisy May *(1954); game over.*

Tennessee, South Carolina and Nevada.

While flipper pinballs couldn't pay out cash awards, some were designed to encourage players to drop in two coins per game. Gottlieb's *Mystic Marvel* (1954) was one of these multiple-replay-award games. If a player inserted two coins at the beginning of the game, all of the replay awards would be doubled. *Mystic Marvel* had several target sequences which would normally award one, two or three replays, so a player could win two, four or even six replays per game with two coins.

Pinball machines of this era used light bulbs behind the backglass to indicate the player's score; as the player hit targets, the lit bulbs would change to advance the score. The player still had to do some addition on his own, though; a score of 2,560,000,

too intricate to easily keep track of more than one player's score. *Super Jumbo* was the first four-player machine, with players taking alternate turns at the game until all of the balls had been played. Scoring on *Super Jumbo* was only in the hundreds (it had only three score reels for each player's score), but players took Gottlieb's new slogan – "It's *More* Fun to Compete" – to heart. Gottlieb called *Super Jumbo* a *perfect multiple-player amusement machine. 1–2–3 or 4 can play at the same time.* Players became more competitive, and *Super Jumbo* was one of the first pinballs to charge ten cents per game rather than a nickel. Gottlieb's first two-player game was *Duette* (1955), again featuring score reels. However, score reels added to the production costs of pinball games, so single-player machines retained the light-up backglass scoring system to keep costs down. In March of 1955, Williams unveiled its first multiple-player game, *Race The Clock*, a four-player machine. During the late fifties, two- and four-player pinballs using score reels became more common. Within two years of Gottlieb's introducing *Miss Annabelle* (1959), its first single-player score reel game, light-

for example, would be indicated by lights on the backglass illuminating a "2 million" panel, a "500,000" panel and a "60,000" panel. This scoring system (which emphasized high-scoring games) changed dramatically in the mid fifties.

Score reels became one of the most important cosmetic changes of the decade. These reels were actually rotating drums, with "0" through "9" printed on them, and they kept score in much the same way as a car's odometer registers mileage. Score reels premiered on shuffle bowling machines produced by United Manufacturing in 1950. Williams experimented with score reels in 1953 on games such as *Gun Club* and *Struggle Buggies*. These games had seven-digit scoring, up to 9,990,000 points, but for some reason, they weren't popular with players, and by 1954, Williams went back to light-up scoring on all of its games.

In October of 1954, Gottlieb released *Super Jumbo*, the company's first game with score reels – and the first machine designed for more than one player. Until 1954, pinball was strictly a one-player game, because the light-up backglass scoring system was

ABOVE High-Diver *featured an animated back glass of rotating divers.*

ABOVE RIGHT *Exhibit Supply Company's* Contact *(1948).*

RIGHT *Williams' 1959* Sea Wolf *featured a disappearing bumper in the center of the playfield.*

up backglass scoring on pinballs had been phased out by all manufacturers.

Not all of the changes in fifties' pinball machines were in the backbox, though — many innovations appeared on the playfields. One of Gottlieb's most popular games of the decade was *Queen Of Hearts* (1952). Designer Wayne Neyens called this game one of his favorites, with its row of five gobble holes. *Queen Of Hearts* offered players several different ways to win replays, all of them tied into ball-to-ball carry-over sequences. Another popular machine was Gottlieb's *Dragonette* (1954). With its satirical art-work (drawn by Roy Parker), *Dragonette's* humorous lampooning of the popular TV show "Dragnet" was a favorite with players. And *Gypsy Queen* (1955) had sixteen rollover lanes, which each lit a different playing card on the backglass; various poker combinations awarded replays.

Williams also had several innovative pinball games in the 1950s. *Nine Sisters* (1953) had only one flipper at the bottom of the playfield, and a strategically placed kickout saucer to save the ball from draining. And Williams" *Hot Diggity* (1956) was a spell-out game: spelling W-A-L-T-Z, T-A-N-G-O or P-O-L-K-A lit

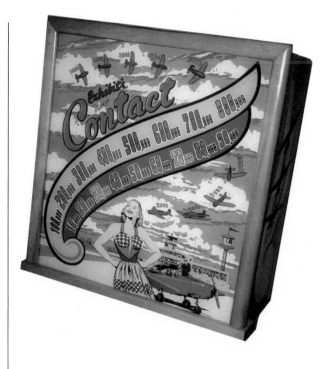

the kickout saucer for a replay, but spelling H-O-T D-I-G-G-I-T-Y lit the kickout saucer for five replays! Williams introduced several new playfield features in the late fifties, including the "Disappearing Bumper." *Gusher* (1958) was the first game with this device, a thumper bumper that could sink below the playfield surface to reveal a high-scoring "special" lane. Disappearing bumpers were only included on two other Williams games because the feature was so expensive to produce.

Bally produced only one flipper game in the 1950s — *Balls-A-Poppin"* (1956), the only two-player machine with light-up backglass scoring. *Balls-A-Poppin"* introduced multiball play, giving players up to six balls on the playfield at once! Bally built only 750 of these machines (a relatively low production run) and waited seven years before introducing its next flipper game in 1963.

The 1950s is sometimes called "The Golden Age of Pinball." Although relatively few new playfield features appeared during this decade, most games had a simple-to-understand layout with easily under-

stood rules. Many pinballs of the fifties had progressive sequences – a series of numbers (or letters or colors) which, when completed, scored "specials." Although pinball was still relegated primarily to pool halls, bowling alleys, taverns and other "shady" locations in this decade, the young post-war baby boom generation was discovering the joys of flipper games. As Gottlieb declared on all of its machines: *Amusement Pinballs – As American As Baseball And Hot Dogs!*

As the 1950s drew to a close, though, pinball seemed to have already peaked. Gottlieb and Williams were turning out a steady stream of games to attract players, but pinball was competing with other popular recreational pastimes, such as wide-screen cinemas and bowling (which was undergoing a surge in popularity). Pinball had gone through an incredible boom after flippers were introduced on *Humpty Dumpty*, and players were looking forward to further innovations that lay ahead for pinball in the 1960s.

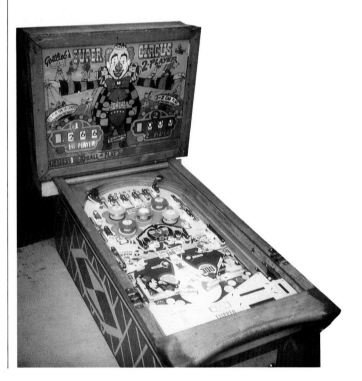

TOP LEFT AND FAR LEFT Gusher; *like* Sea Wolf, *this machine had a bumper that could be made to rise and fall as appropriate by the skilled player.*

LEFT Super Circus *from Gottlieb (1957); note the curved wooden top rail at the player's end.*

ABOVE *Circus themes are a great excuse for a riot of colour, as on this Genco machine of 1949.*

THE GROWING YEARS
(1960-77)

A s the 1960s dawned, pinball was fighting to attract players. Competition from coin-operated bowling machines and other arcade games had drawn away many pinball players, and only two manufacturers were still producing pinball machines. These were Gottlieb and Williams, who continued to explore new design ideas, in their efforts to lure back the players who had flocked to pinball only a few years earlier.

Score reels were becoming more common on pinball machines, because two- and four-player games encouraged competition among players. Most single-player games of 1960 and 1961 still had light-up backglass scoring, although these were rapidly being replaced by the more modern-looking score reels. In the summer of 1960, Williams unveiled *Darts*, a single-player pinball (with light-up back-glass scoring) featuring a "magnificent new cabinet design" which "meets the challenge of the 60's," according to the company. *Darts* had a streamlined appearance with its tubular metal legs and "recessed cigarette and drink shelf" with "dual sloping fins," according to the company's promotional material. This new design never caught on with players, though, and less than a year after its "Styling of the 60's" design premiered, Williams returned to a more traditional look on its games.

At about the same time, Gottlieb went in a different (and much more successful) direction to attract players. Late in 1960, "add-a-ball" play was introduced on a game designed by Wayne Neyens called *Flipper*. Instead of awarding replays for high scores, *Flipper* extended the length of the game by awarding additional balls instead of free games, so a player could continue the game as long as he could win additional balls (most add-a-ball games could register up to ten balls yet to play). *Flipper* was a

RIGHT Flipper *was designed by Wayne Neyens, and was the first add-a-ball game.*

OPPOSITE Darts *was felt to be very avant-garde in its artwork when released in 1960.*

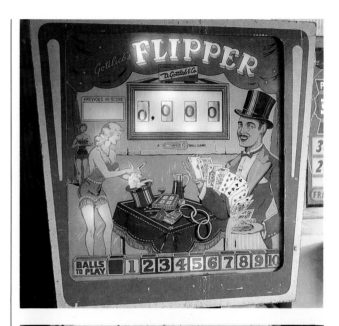

breakthrough in pinball, inspired by Alvin Gottlieb. After being branded as gambling for many years because of the replay unit, *Flipper* was a game that was acceptable to many critics because of its add-a-ball play. According to a company press release, Flipper *has no provisions for free play. The spectacular new add-a-ball feature gives the player the thrill of extended play and a feeling of accomplishment that is equivalent to the attraction of free plays.* Flipper combined two of pinball's most popular themes – cards and magic – into a game which satisfied both players and pinball critics. Add-a-ball games remain popular with many players even today, and are still the only type of pinballs allowed in some areas. *Flipper* was such an overwhelming success that Gottlieb produced a string of similarly named games to emphasize their add-a-ball appeal – *Flipper Parade* (1961), *Flipper Fair* (1961), *Flipper Clown*

51

(1962) and *Flipper Cowboy* (1962).

New playfield features were also surfacing at this time. One of the most popular of these made its first appearance on Williams' *Vagabond* (1962). In the center of *Vagabond's* playfield was a small rectangular target which would "drop" beneath the playfield's surface when it was hit. "Drop targets" were an instant hit with players and are still one of the most popular playfield features today. Interestingly, it wasn't until 1971's *Groovy* that Gottlieb included drop targets on a game. Bally also waited until the early seventies to introduce drop targets on their games.

Beat The Clock (1963) was another landmark Williams game which revived multiball play, tried only once before on Bally's *Balls-A-Poppin'* (1956). *Beat The Clock* had a kickout saucer to trap the ball. Once trapped, the ball remained in the saucer while

ABOVE LEFT *The back box on this Williams game is the same shape as on Gottlieb games, but inverted.*
LEFT *Flipper Clown was an early* example of an add-a-ball game.
BELOW *Animation has always helped to sell a game; on Central Park the monkey signals a replay by striking the bell.*

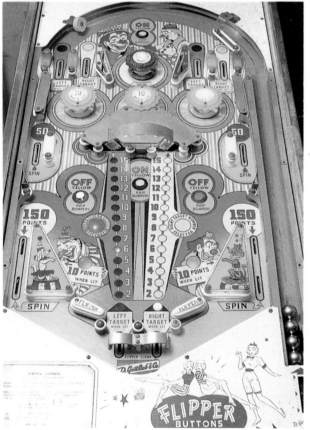

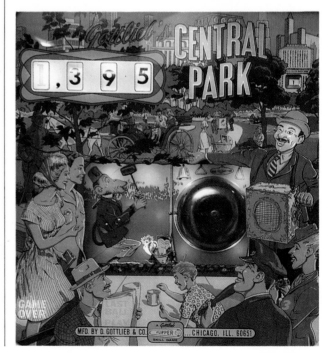

another ball was delivered to the plunger for the player to shoot. If the second ball landed in another saucer or passed through the top rollover lane, the first ball would be released. By keeping both balls on the playfield together, the player could score a replay.

Another popular playfield feature was also unveiled in 1963. Gottlieb's *Swing Along* introduced spinners (also called "spinning targets," "swinging targets" and "spinning flags"). These thin, metal rectangles were suspended perpendicular to the playfield, and would spin around when hit by the ball; the harder they were hit, the more points would be scored. Players enjoyed seeing the spinning action and hearing the ringing chimes that would be activated. Spinners are still used on many of today's games.

While these and other new playfield devices were appearing, an older feature was being phased out. Gottlieb's *Sweet Hearts* (1963), released about the same time as *Swing Along*, marked the final appearance of gobble holes, once common on many pinballs of the 1950s and early sixties, especially on Gottlieb games. Although gobble holes often awarded replays or high scores, they also abruptly ended a player's ball. By the mid sixties, many players were

already accustomed to add-a-ball play, and were more interested in longer-playing games than receiving free games.

By 1963, pinball was popular again and players were sampling many new playfield features. Chicago Coin, which had left the pinball field for most of the fifties to concentrate on producing arcade games, returned with *Sun Valley* (1963), *Firecracker* (1963) and *Bronco* (1963). Keeney, once a leader in pinball production during the 1930s and forties, unveiled its first pinball since 1953 – *Poker Face* (1963), followed by *Go Cart* (1963), *Arrowhead* (1963) and *Colorama* (1963). A newcomer to the pinball world was Midway Manufacturing. In 1963, this five-year-old company unveiled *Race Way*, which had a rather ordinary play-field design but a very unusual scoring system. *Race Way* featured two miniature racing cars in the back-box, positioned on an oval track. Hitting selected playfield targets caused these cars to move ahead various distances, and scored points for completing

ABOVE LEFT *Early sixties Gottlieb games could display a "score to beat".*

BELOW Sweet Hearts *in the* Freight Train *coffee bar, in swinging London, 1963.*

laps. A follow-up to *Race Way*, *Flying Turns* (1964), used the same gimmick, although Midway's final pinball, *Rodeo* (1964), was a more conventional game.

But the most significant entry into the pinball market in 1963 was Bally. After producing only one flipper game in the 1950s (*Balls-A-Poppin'*), Bally unveiled *Moon Shot* and suddenly Gottlieb and Williams had a new competitor. *Moon Shot* was the first pinball designed by Ted Zale, formerly an engineer with Genco who came to Bally in the early sixties to work on arcade games. When Bally had a major management change in 1963 and decided to resume pinball production, Zale found himself the company's sole pinball designer. Zale decided that the best way for Bally to attract players would be to design games that were radically different from the symmetrical layouts by Gottlieb and Williams. Zale's games often featured asymmetrical playfields with unusual arrangements of ball gates. One of his inventions was the "mushroom bumper," a cylindrical scoring device which became his unofficial trademark. Mushroom bumpers were included on nearly every pinball produced by Bally in the sixties after their first appearance on *Monte Carlo* (1964). Like

BELOW Poker Face *at the distributors, November 1963.*

ABOVE Moon Shot *and* Tropic Isle;
*the latter included an illuminated
monkey which ascended the palm
tree as the score progressed.*

Gottlieb and Williams, Bally pinballs have remained in constant production.

Over at Williams, designer Steven Kordek was joined by Norman Clark, whose first game was *King Pin* (1962), a bowling-theme game which featured 10 rollover buttons (arranged like bowling pins) in the center of the playfield. *King Pin* also had a "kickup shooter" between the flippers, which shot the ball back into play.

Wayne Neyens was still Gottlieb's chief pinball designer in the early sixties. Many of his playfields featured several "pop bumpers" designed to add random action to the game. Neyens designed *Slick Chick* (1963), which had nine bumpers lettered S-L-I-C-K-C-H-I-C-K; hitting all these bumpers spelled out the name of the game and lit the center gobble

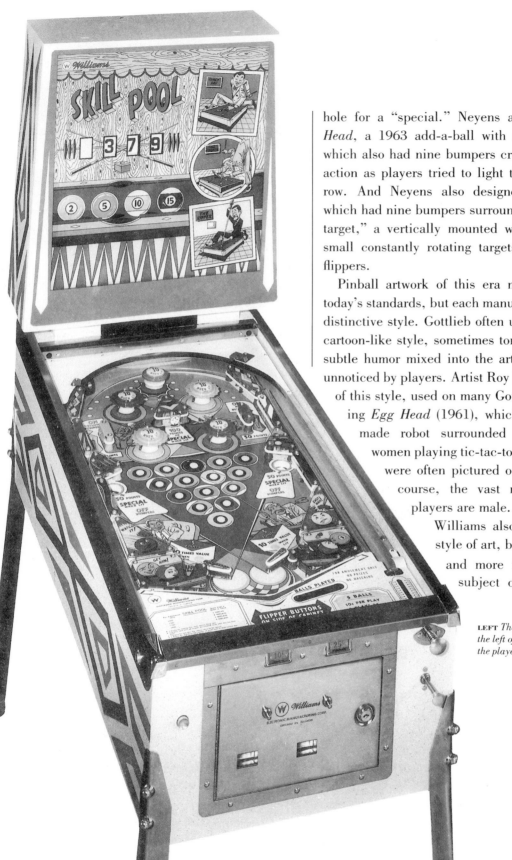

hole for a "special." Neyens also created *Square Head*, a 1963 add-a-ball with a tic-tac-toe motif, which also had nine bumpers creating constant ball action as players tried to light three Xs or Os in a row. And Neyens also designed *Goucho* (1963), which had nine bumpers surrounding a centre "roto-target," a vertically mounted wheel with only two small constantly rotating targets accessible to the flippers.

Pinball artwork of this era may seem dated by today's standards, but each manufacturer had its own distinctive style. Gottlieb often used an exaggerated cartoon-like style, sometimes tongue-in-cheek, with subtle humor mixed into the artwork that might go unnoticed by players. Artist Roy Parker was a master of this style, used on many Gottlieb games including *Egg Head* (1961), which pictured a home-made robot surrounded by several young women playing tic-tac-toe. Attractive women were often pictured on pinball games: of course, the vast majority of pinball players are male.

Williams also used a cartoonish style of art, but with less subtlety and more focus on the main subject of the art.

LEFT *The "blank" on* Skill Pool *to the left of the score reels lit up when the player's score reached 1,000.*

ABOVE *The object of* Grand Tour *was to "visit" the capital cities, which then lit up on the back glass.*

RIGHT *The wholesome C & W kitsch of Bally's* Harvest.

"advance" bumpers on the playfield caused the "temperature" to rise, lighting the drop target for a replay.

While this animation was fascinating to many players, it was also predictable. By looking at the backglass, players knew that *Flipper Parade's* animation unit would fire a cannonball. In the mid sixties, a new dimension in animation was explored when comical suspense was added. Players could tell that some gag would be revealed through the animation, but they couldn't learn the punch line without playing the machine themselves (or watching someone else play). Gottlieb's *Skyline* (1965) had an animated elevator in the backglass; if the player hit the proper targets, the elevator doors would open to reveal a crowd of people squeezed inside. *Masquerade* (1966) was another Gottlieb game which featured a girl holding a fan in front of her face; spelling out M-A-S-K-E-D-B-E-A-U-T-Y closed the fan, revealing her face. And Gottlieb's *Crosstown* (1966) pictured a crowded subway car waiting in a station; players

Williams backglasses of the early sixties left an immediate impression on players. Because of all the intricate detail in Gottlieb artwork, a player might notice something new each time he looked at the same backglass, while Williams" more direct style immediately focused the player's attention on a central image. Bally used a slightly more realistic style, but if there was a similarity in the artwork of all three manufacturers, it was because the same company, Advertising Posters of Chicago (under the direction of George Molentin) handled the artistic duties for all these manufacturers.

Pinball machines continued attracting attention in the sixties through the use of three-dimensional animation in the backglasses. Gottlieb's *Flipper Parade* (1961) featured a drawing of a cannon on the backglass which fired a small "cannonball" whenever the player was awarded an extra ball. Gottlieb's *Flipper Cowboy* (1962) included a revolving target in the backbox, activated whenever an extra ball was scored. And Williams' *Heat Wave* (1964) had an animated thermometer in the backglass; hitting

could open the subway's animated doors, revealing a massive crowd of passengers jammed together.

Sometimes elaborate animation just wasn't practical. One of Williams' most popular pinballs of the 1960s was *Magic City* (1967), with artwork picturing a beautiful fountain in the center of a plush, bustling metropolis. Designer Norman Clark tried incorporating a rotating color wheel in the backbox behind the fountain for a bubbling three-dimensional effect, but the feature proved too expensive and was never included on the game.

During the 1960s, designing a pinball game was almost a solo effort. Except for the artwork, the designer created the playfield layout, developed the game rules and even did most of the inside wiring. A designer needed mechanical aptitude along with creativity, and if he had an idea for a new playfield feature, it was up to him to develop it himself rather than depend on someone else to put it together. One of the most significant mechanical developments in pinball was the "split bank," invented by Clark for his 1966 *Eight Ball* game. *Eight Ball* had a pool motif, with players trying to light 15 numbers scattered around the playfield, as in a real game. Carrying over lit targets from ball to ball was a simple matter on single-player machines, but because *Eight*

Ball was a two-player game, keeping track of which targets a player had hit posed a problem. Clark's split bank provided a rudimentary "memory" on the game, one of the very few multiple-player mechanical pinball machines able to retain playfield status. Clark reused the split bank concept on Williams' *Solids 'N Stripes* (1970), another pool-theme game.

Another feature invented by Clark was the up-post – a lighted, cylinder-shaped object that popped up between the flippers to prevent the ball from draining. Clark included up-posts on many of his games, among them *Cabaret* (1969), *Doodle Bug* (1971) and *Gold Rush* (1971).

Still another Clark invention was the captive ball spinner unit, actually a sort of mini roulette wheel,

ABOVE LEFT Magic City, *a sixties classic combining satisfying "skill shots" and colorful design.*

BELOW *The bumper between the flippers gives the skillful player the opportunity to display "graunching" skills.*

58

which premiered on Williams' *A-Go-Go* (1966). This device had a marble-sized ball contained in a spinner in the center of the playfield which awarded bonus points. Clark reused this feature on *Suspense* (1969). Gottlieb included a similar captive ball spinner on its 1967 *Hi-Score* game.

By the mid 1960s, add-a-ball games had opened many areas to pinball where it had previously been outlawed. While the early add-a-ball games had original playfield designs created especially for add-a-ball play, later games had playfields identical to replay models, but with different (although similar) names. For instance, Gottlieb's *Buckaroo* and *Cowpoke* (1965) were identical, except that *Buckaroo* awarded replays, while players could win only extra balls on *Cowpoke*. Other replay/add-a-ball combinations of the 1960s include *Bank-A-Ball* and *Flipper Pool* (1965), *Ice Revue* and *Ice Show* (1966), *King of Diamonds* and *Diamond Jack* (1967) and *Royal Guard* and *Palace Guard* (1968), all by Gottlieb. Williams also produced add-a-ball games similar to their replay counterparts, including 1964's *Zig-Zag* (replay) and *Wing Ding* (add-a-ball), *Lucky Strike* and *Bowl-A-Strike* (1965), *Full House* and *Top Hand* (1966) and *Blast Off* and *Apollo* (1967). (There is a full description of Apollo's beauties in play and appearance in Chapter 7.) Add-a-ball machines were produced by every manufacturer until 1977, when mechanical games were replaced by electronic pinballs which were adjustable to either format.

In 1966, Bally designer Ted Zale invented a feature that some players thought would revolutionize pinball when it was unveiled on a 1966 game called *Bazaar*. This feature was named "zipper flippers." When you hit the proper target, the flippers would move together, closing the flipper gap. *Bazaar* was a popular game, but as a single-player machine, it received only limited exposure. The real test for zipper flippers came with Zale's next design, a four-player game that featured not only zipper flippers but also a new twist on a previously tried game idea.

ABOVE AND BELOW *The animated back glass of* Crosstown *featured subway doors which opened and* closed when a replay was awarded. The add-a-ball version was called Subway.

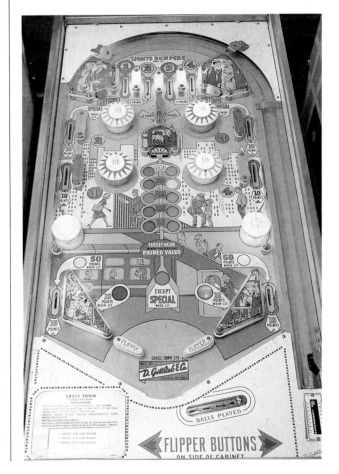

ABOVE Royal Guard *was the add-a-ball variant of the replay version,* Palace Guard. *Swinging London gets the treatment again.*

Ice Revue *was the replay version of add-a-ball* Ice Show; *the skates on the back glass were illuminated individually.*

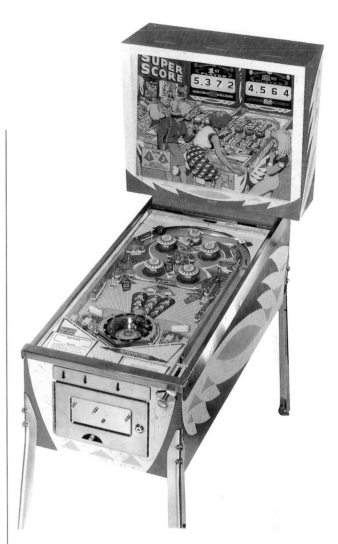

Bally finally produced its first big hit game – *Capersville* – following *Bazaar*. *Capersville* revived multi-ball play, but went a step further than Williams' *Beat The Clock* by featuring a three-ball multiball game. If a player locked the ball in one of the two top kickout saucers, a second ball appeared by the plunger. If this second ball was trapped in the remaining saucer, a third ball appeared, and all three balls could be released simultaneously. *Capersville* also had a colorful backglass along with its zipper flippers. Bally built a company-record 5,120 *Capersvilles*, dwarfing the usual 500–2,000 production runs which the company had had on most of its games in the preceding three years.

Pinball themes varied widely in the 1960s, although each designer had his own personal favorites: Williams' Steven Kordek was partial to outer space motifs, for example. Gottlieb was considered the "king" of card games, turning out machines such as 1963's *Sweet Hearts* (billed as "A Smash Hit from the Master-Maker of Card Games!"), *Kings & Queens* (1965) and *King of Diamonds* (1967). Pool was also a popular subject for pinball, on games including Bally's *Cue Tease* (1964), Gottlieb's *Target Pool* (1969) and Williams' *Cue-T* (1969).

One of the most interesting subjects was illustrated on a 1967 Williams game called *Beat Time*. The backglass pictured four young musicians called "The Bootles." The playfield design was rather unremarkable, although the game commands a high price today because of its artwork (it's in especially high demand at gatherings of Beatles fans).

By the end of the decade, a major design change was taking place on pinball games. The small two-inch flippers that had been used on games since 1947's *Humpty Dumpty* were slowly being replaced with longer three-inch flippers. The first appearance of these longer flippers was on Williams' *Hayburners II* (1968), a horse-racing game designed by Steven Kordek. *Hayburners II* had no plunger – the ball was launched from between the flippers – and these longer

ABOVE Super Score *featured a roulette wheel between the flippers and depicted other Gottlieb pintables on the back glass.*

flippers (which closed up like Bally's zipper flippers) were ideally suited to the game. Williams returned to short flippers on its next few games until *Suspense* (1969), which included two sets of flippers – one long pair and one short pair. After *Suspense*, Williams used short flippers only as "extra flippers" in the center of the playfield, relying entirely on long flippers for the main set at the bottom of the playfield. Gottlieb introduced three-inch flippers in 1970 on *Play Ball*, a baseball-theme game, with the longer flippers conspicuously labeled "Bat" so players would feel comfortable with them. Chicago Coin, though, went to an extreme when it unveiled *Big Flipper* in 1970, sporting a pair of five-inch flippers! In 1971, Chicago Coin adopted three-inch flippers like the other

ABOVE Fireball Classic *is a remake of Bally's extremely successful original electromechanical game (see page 105), using microchip technology.*

artwork. *Four Million BC* (1971) was outstanding in pinball art, and introduced players to some new ideas in pinball design.

Although players had never flocked to play Bally pinballs, *Four Million BC* changed all that. *Four Million BC* had a prehistoric theme, with playfield features called "The Volcano" and the "Tar Pit." Ted

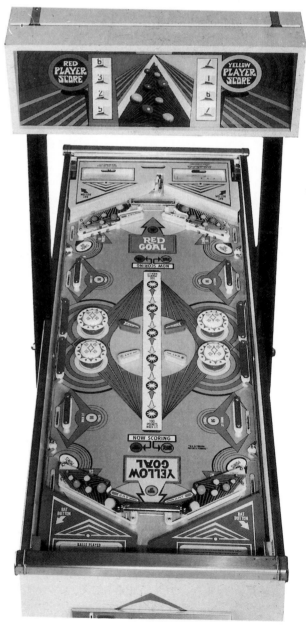

manufacturers.

In the late 1960s, pinball artwork also began to change, especially on Williams' games. Many of the drawings became very angular; the characters had long, pointy arms and legs, with triangular shapes becoming common. Some outstanding examples of this artistic style include *Solids 'N Stripes* (1970), *Stardust* (1972) and *Gulfstream* (1973).

Although some of Bally's games had utilized this angular style, including *Firecracker* (1971), *Four Queens* (1971) and *Mariner* (1972), other Bally pinballs used a more detailed, realistic approach to

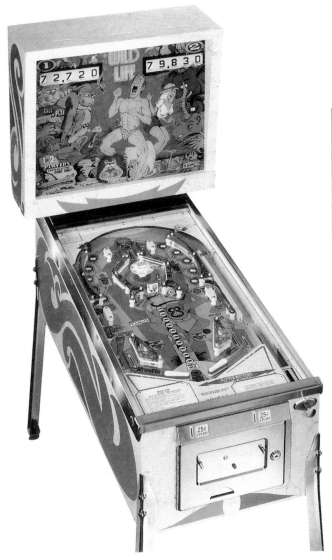

famous artists (see Chapter 7 for an account of his work), was new to the pinball world but his first game has become one of the most sought-after pinball machines by collectors – Bally's *Fireball* (1972). The backglass pictured a mythical, red man-like monster hurling fireballs toward the player. This character also appeared on the playfield surrounded by the "Fire Gods" kickout saucers – Odin and Wotan, two captive ball holes on either side of the playfield. If a player shot his ball into one of these saucers, it would remain trapped and a second ball would appear by the plunger. The player could then try to release the trapped ball by hitting the proper mushroom bumper, or could trap a second ball in the remaining saucer on the way to three-ball multiball play. *Fireball* also had a spinning disc (sometimes called a "whirlwind spinner") in the center of the playfield which would send the ball spinning in unpredictable directions; even the best player might find the ball flung out of play between the flippers with no warning. *Fireball* also had a "captive messenger ball" – a pinball permanently trapped in an enclosed channel on the playfield, which scored points if hit by the player's ball. And to top it off, *Fireball* even had zipper flippers, which may have seemed a bit "dated" to players because of their small size, since all pinball

LEFT *Two players play simultaneously from each end on* Challenger, *which makes Body English quite intriguing! Note the vertical arrangement of the scores.*

ABOVE Wild Life *featured a "ball kicker gate" which could send*

the ball back into play from the left exit lane.

RIGHT High Score Pool *from Chicago Dynamic Industries, a company not quite in the super league of the Big Three – Bally, Williams and Gottlieb.*

Zale had designed a unique plunger shot on the game, with the ball coming out of the plunger lane at midfield only to cross over to the upper left side of the game. *Four Million BC* was also a three-ball multiball game, again featuring zipper flippers. It was an extremely popular game, proving that a radically different multiball design could succeed.

The following year, Bally released another pinball with a different style of artwork that again attracted players. David Christensen, one pinball's most

games had been designed with longer flippers for about two years. *Fireball* was an instant hit, and 3,815 were produced, ranking it as the second highest production Bally pinball game ever (only *Capersville* topped *Fireball*). *Fireball* was one of Zale's last games, and certainly his most famous. *Fireball* is one of the few pinball games that could be worth more now than when it was produced, with near-mint *Fireballs* sometimes fetching upward of $1,000 today.

In 1973, Bally unveiled still another popular game, *Nip-It*. This fishing-theme pinball featured

LEFT Big Injun, *which was also marketed as* Big Brave *(two player) and* Big Indian *(four player).*

ABOVE Travel time, *designed by Norm Clark, gave the player an unlimited number of balls, but a time limit which could be extended with good scoring. It was also manufactured by Segasa in Spain.*

two-ball multiball, a kickback lane and zipper flippers, but its most unusual feature was the "Gator Grabber." This new playfield device was a metal bar located in the upper right corner of the playfield, activated by an extra button on the side of the cabinet next to the right flipper button. The Gator Grabber could swing over the ball, manipulating it into a high-scoring lane. *Nip-It* was great fun to play, and after the success of *Four Million BC* and *Fireball*, established Bally as an innovative pinball manufacturer.

Some very unusual pinball machines were also appearing at this time. One of the strangest was Gottlieb's 1971 *Challenger*, a two-player, head-to-head game. *Challenger* was a two-sided machine, with players standing at each end, facing each other, each controlling a set of flippers. The object was to maneuver the ball into the opposing player's "goal" between the flippers. *Challenger* was eye-catching, although the playfield offered few targets, since the strategy was geared toward directing the ball into the "goal" area rather than scoring points. *Challenger's*

main drawback, though, was that two people were needed to play the game. Reportedly, less than 500 *Challengers* were built.

Another pinball variation was produced in 1971 – Chicago Coin's *Hi-Score Pool*. Instead of the usual layout of targets and bumpers, *Hi-Score Pool* simply had an array of 15 "pool balls" and a pair of flippers. The pool balls were suspended over the playfield, and players tried guiding the pinball beneath each of the pool balls. *Hi-Score Pool* was designed primarily for add-a-ball areas, although the concept was too awkward for most players to feel comfortable with.

Chicago Coin's conventional pinballs were never popular with players, although several of them had interesting layouts and unusual features. *Casino* (1973) picked up the spinning-disc idea from Bally's *Fireball* and included two whirlwind spinners on the playfield. And *Dolphin* (1974) featured three captive

BELOW Superstar *had a kicker hole blocked by a drop target, a device used first on* Honey, *designed by Steve Kordek.*

ABOVE RIGHT Sea Hunt *was the first "shakerball" game; advertised with the slogan "TILT is a four-letter word".*

messenger balls in the center of the playfield. Although Chicago Coin produced two or three different pinballs each year from 1963 until the mid 1970s (when the company was sold to Stern Electronics), they somehow never produced any really outstanding games.

A small Florida-based manufacturer, Allied Leisure Industries, unveiled another radically different pinball machine in 1972 – *Sea Hunt*. The game, Allied's first pinball, was housed in a vertical cabinet, and had a much smaller than normal playfield. Players operated the flippers by using two vertical joysticks on the front of the cabinet rather than using buttons; these joysticks could also move the entire playfield up and down slightly, so Allied dubbed *Sea Hunt* a "shakerball" machine. The following year, Allied

Sometimes, last-minute production changes were made on machines. Gottlieb's *Big Injun* (1973) was popular with players, but before the game went into production, Gottlieb realized that the word "Injun" had derogatory connotations, and the game was changed to *Big Indian*.

In 1973, a new type of coin-operated game began attracting players' attention. Video games had just appeared, and players were fascinated with these TV games which simulated ping-pong action. Interestingly enough, pinball was also attracting more players than ever at the same time. Coin-op amusement games of all types were becoming "respectable," and all three of the major manufacturers were turning out popular pinballs to keep players happy.

Gottlieb's *Orbit* (1972) went over big with players. *Orbit* featured a "vari-target," a small metal bar that scored a variable number of points depending upon how hard it was hit by the ball. *Jack In The Box* (1972) was another popular favorite, as players tried to knock down a row of 10 drop targets. And

LEFT Dealer's Choice, *designed by Norm Clark, had a wide-open playfield which allowed long skill shots and fast action. Notice the unusual flipper layout.*

BELOW Space Mission – *a Steve Kordek classic from Williams – has the highest production run to date.*

produced another shakerball called *Spooksville*, although by this time the novelty had worn thin.

Williams' *Travel Time* (1973) was also unusual because the game was based on time rather than a set number of balls. Players would begin with 60 units on the clock, which would tick away as the game progressed. Players could stop the clock and add additional seconds for extended play, but when the clock reached zero, the game was over. *Travel Time* did especially well in add-a-ball areas, although the machine could also be set to award replays.

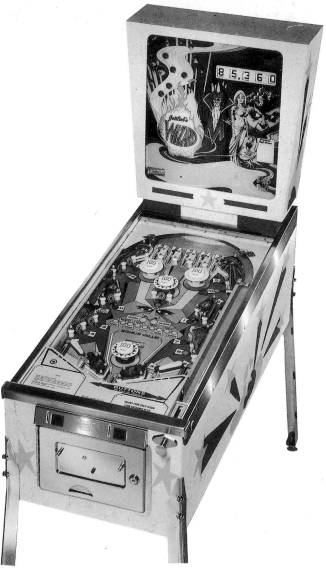

Gottlieb's *Big Indian* had a little bit of everything — a vari-target, a bank of five drop targets and a line of three rollover buttons, along with usual array of bumpers and rollover lanes.

Williams was also turning out some excellent games. *Spanish Eyes* (1972), designed by Norman Clark, had a large, open-ended horseshoe-shaped lane in the center of the playfield, but the game is most remembered for its unusual placement of a thumper bumper between the flippers. *Fun Fest* (1973) featured a swinging target in the center of the play-field; designed by Steven Kordek, this target moved slowly from side to side, requiring the player to both aim and time his shot. Another of Kordek's games, *Jubilee* (1973), featured five captive balls held in a U-shaped enclosure in the center of the playfield; hitting the balls from one side of the enclosure to the other scored bonus points, extra balls and replays. One of Williams' most popular machines was a game called *OXO* (1973). Players tried lighting Xs and Os in a grid in the center of the playfield by hitting selected targets (and avoiding others).

Bally was also producing some popular games as well, including designer Jim Patla's *Boomerang* (1973), which featured two captive messenger balls and a single thumper bumper surrounded by a rebound ring. *Air Aces* (1975) was another hit Bally game with its line-up of 10 drop targets and extra set of small flippers.

By early 1975, pinball was so popular that it became the subject of a movie. The film *Tommy*, starring the rock band The Who with Roger Daltrey as the "deaf, dumb and blind kid" who "sure plays a mean pinball," threw pinball into a national spotlight. The Who's song "Pinball Wizard" became a top ten hit, and reminded an entire generation of youthful

TOP RIGHT *Super-Flite was also marketed as* Strato-flite, *a four-player game.*

RIGHT *Gottlieb's* Wizard — *not to be confused with the famous Bally game of the same name — was only sold in Italy.*

players about the joy of playing pinball.

Later that year, Bally unveiled the first mega-hit pinball, *Wizard*. The artwork, created by David Christensen (of *Fireball* fame), was based on *Tommy*, with two of the film's stars (Roger Daltrey and Ann-Margret) pictured on the backglass. It was a striking design which instantly attracted anyone who had seen *Tommy*, along with people who had missed the film but were fascinated by the artwork. Playfield designer Greg Kmiec had created a superb layout centered around four "flip flags" which awarded double bonus and increased the playfield's scoring values. Longtime Williams pinball designer Norman Clark had taken over as the head of Bally's pinball design department, and *Wizard* was one of the first games produced under his guidance. *Wizard* was the first Bally game to break the 10,000 mark in production (10,005 were built), but it had a much more important impact on pinball games, because for the first time, the importance of a popular theme was evident. Nearly every arcade had a *Wizard*, and most placed them next to the door to attract players.

Bally wasn't the only company riding high, though. Williams was also dazzling players with *Space Mission* (1975), one of its most successful games ever. Designer Steven Kordek included a spinner lane, a

bonus horseshoe, swinging target and more in a game picturing the US-Soviet space link-up of 1975. Kordek, always partial to space-themed machines, said *Space Mission* was inspired by a trip he made to Europe, where he saw the excitement generated by space exploration, and added that the artwork was based on actual NASA photographs. Williams' promotional material called *Space Mission A far out game with the most tantalizing, exciting, play-inviting, appealing playfield gadgetry ever presented for play-again action.*

Gottlieb's *Spirit of 76* (1976) was also a big favorite with players. The theme was based on the US bicentennial celebration and pictured a frontier pioneer beside an astronaut, while the playfield included eight drop targets marked 1-7-7-6 and 1-9-7-6. *Spirit Of 76* was a fast-playing game, and like Bally's *Wizard*, more than 10,000 were produced. Gottlieb's *Royal Flush* was another popular card-themed game which featured a long bank of drop targets and a single thumper bumper. *Surf Champ* (1976) was

ABOVE LEFT *The striking and unusual geometric art work of Williams'* Spanish Eyes.

BELOW Casino *featured two whirlwind spinners.*

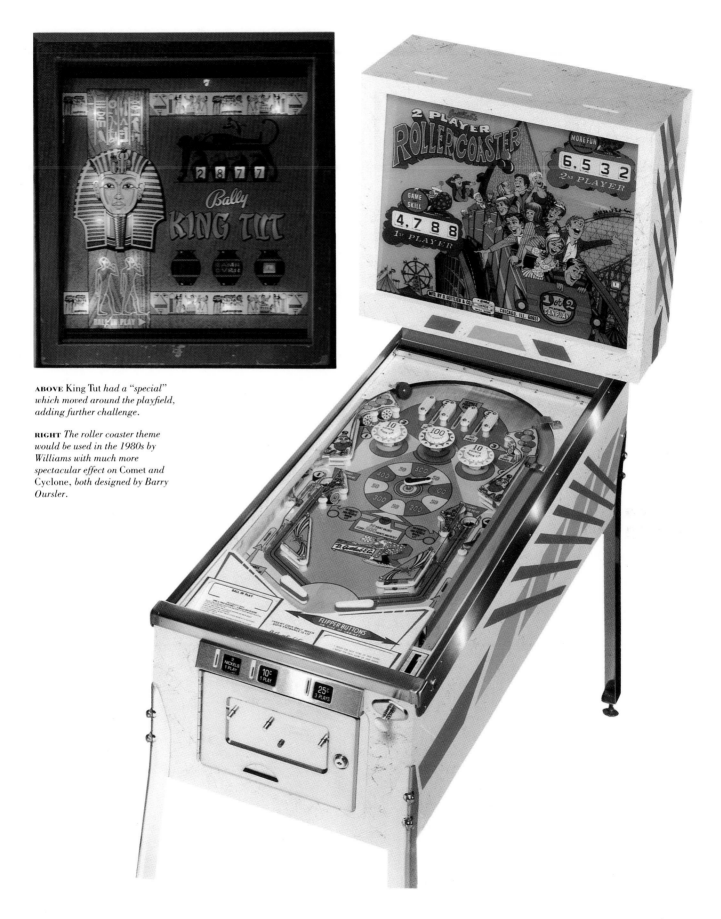

ABOVE King Tut *had a "special" which moved around the playfield, adding further challenge.*

RIGHT *The roller coaster theme would be used in the 1980s by Williams with much more spectacular effect on* Comet *and* Cyclone, *both designed by Barry Oursler.*

LEFT Soccer *was a two-player game with soccer-ball animation.*

ABOVE Triple Strike, *like* Wild Card *(right) had six-digit scoring.*

OPPOSITE *Notice how far the playfield has developed on games like* Wild Card *(designed by Steve Kordek) in comparison with the uncomplicated symmetry of earlier games.*

another Gottlieb loaded with features – a drop target bank, rollover buttons, spinner, kickout saucer, triple bonus and more.

Bally's *Old Chicago* (1976), designed by Greg Kmiec, was another hit. The backglass pictured John Dillinger with two beautiful gun molls, done in an eye-catching shade of pink. More than 7,000 *Old Chicagos* were produced, but it was Bally's next game that really proved that pinball was here to stay.

Captain Fantastic (1976) was another *Tommy*-inspired game picturing Elton John as pinball champ Captain Fantastic. David Christensen again did the artwork for this Bally game, using a lot of bright reds and blues. Piano keyboards (Elton John's favorite instrument) appeared throughout the game, which was one of the first featuring custom-designed bumpers caps with drawings of Elton John's face. The backglass pictured a crowd scene based on *Tommy*; Christensen cleverly hid the faces of some of his friends in the drawings, and even pictured Hitler in the crowd! *Captain Fantastic* also had mirror lines

worked into the backglass art for a dazzling reflective effect. Greg Kmiec created the playfield design, which had a pleasing, uncluttered arrangement of targets and bumpers, plus four flippers. *Captain Fantasic* had a simple, appealing layout coupled with a popular theme and artwork. Bally built a record 16,155 *Captain Fantastics*, and now, well over a decade later, some of these machines are still in use.

Williams introduced *Grand Prix* in 1977. Designed by Steven Kordek, it had an auto racing theme, two bonus systems and *steady, unpredictable, intriguing*

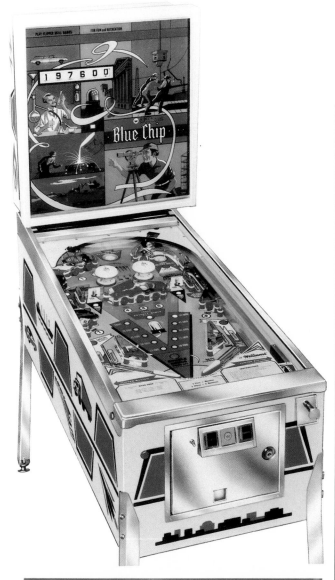

ball action on a playfield designed to capture and hold the interest from the advance bonus kick-out hole at the top to collect bonus time when the ball leaves the playfield, according to the sales brochure. And Williams' *Big Deal* (1977) featured two drop-target banks and horseshoe turnaround.

Players were also enjoying such Gottlieb games as *Target Alpha* (1977). This futuristic-themed game had an unusual ball shooter entry that directed the ball straight to the center of the playfield, where the player could shoot for any of the 15 drop targets. *Jungle Queen* was another 1977 Gottlieb game that was a hit with players. *Jungle Queen* boasted four flippers – two large and two small – designed to aim the ball at the twin drop target banks on either side of the playfield.

But a revolution in pinball had already started, as electronic games had begun appearing in the mid seventies. First Bally, then Williams and Gottlieb, began producing these solid state machines, though Gottlieb continued making electromechanical pinballs through most of 1978, as some players felt more comfortable with the familiar score reels than with electronic numbers. *Golden Arrow* and *Strange World* were two 1978 single-player mechanical pinballs produced by Gottlieb. In an effort to broaden the games' appeal, Gottlieb even created a mechanical pinball disguised to look like an electronic game! *Hit The Deck* (1978) was a single-player mechanical machine, but its score reels were black (rather than white), with the numbers printed in red computerlike digits. The trick didn't fool many players.

A new era in pinball was dawning, and exciting possibilities lay ahead. While the end of the mechanical pinball era was at hand, pinball was experiencing a boom in its popularity which ensured that flipper games would be around for a long time to come.

FAR LEFT Blue Chip *(designed by Steve Horlick) was the first game to use the new jet bumper.*

FAR LEFT, BELOW Toledo *was a personal favorite of designer Harry Williams. "It's more fun to compete"; it also keeps the money rolling in.*

ABOVE AND LEFT Liberty Bell, *designed by Steve Kordek, celebrated the Bicentennial.*

THE ELECTRONIC AGE
(1975-88)

*I*n the 1970s microchip technology was sweeping the world. Pocket calculators, watches and even bathroom scales began utilizing newly developed microprocessors; pinball machines were particularly suited to their application, and were thus in the vanguard of the new science.

The first digital pinball, called *Spirit Of 76*, appeared in mid 1975 (not to be confused with Gottlieb's of the following year). Produced by Mirco Games, a small company in Phoenix, Arizona, it stood apart from other games because the familiar scoring reels had been replaced with electronic numbers. Other changes were made inside the machine too, with tiny microchips now handling the work that once was performed by a dozen relay banks and yards of wire. *Spirit Of 76* was the first pinball machine produced by Mirco, a company which had built its reputation on table soccer and video games. While the digital scoring was interesting, the playfield design and artwork left much to be desired. Only about 100 *Spirit Of 76* games were produced, as everyone waited for digital scoring to be applied to a more "exciting" game. By the end of the year, all the pinball manufacturers were experimenting with their own digital pinball games, vying with each other to

be first to perfect the technology.

Early in 1976, Allied Leisure Industries introduced *Dyn-O-Mite*, and the digital pinball market exploded. *Dyn-O-Mite* combined new playfield features such as disappearing drop targets with artwork based on the hit TV show *Good Times* starring Jimmie Walker. The result was a game that was not only fun to play but also had "space age" digital scoring. Players lined up around *Dyn-O-Mite* and a new era in pinball began. Unfortunately, Allied was a small pinball manufacturer with a poor reputation for quality control. While players were delighted with the digital scoring, arcade owners weren't happy with Allied's track record and most decided to wait for an electronic pinball game from one of the "big" manufacturers.

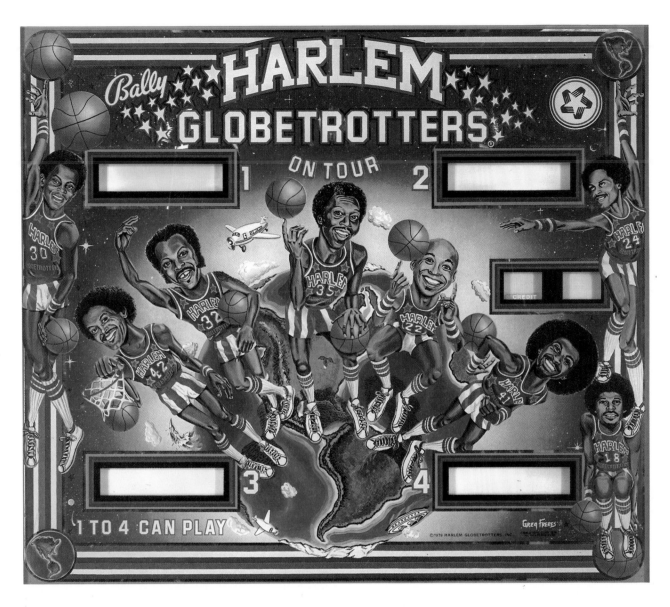

It wasn't long before industry leader Bally began producing its own digital pinballs. By the end of the year, Bally's *Freedom* and *Night Rider* games appeared in both mechanical and electronic versions. The other pinball companies also began turning out electronic pinballs soon after, but it was Bally who dominated the pinball scene, outselling all of its competitors combined by three-to-one.

Solid state technology opened new frontiers in pinball design. One of the greatest limitations of older mechanical pins was the scorekeeping; the score reels could turn only so fast, and if the ball hit two targets in rapid succession, the scoring on the second target would be lost because the first target's points would still be registering. However, electronic pinballs could

FAR LEFT Bow and Arrow *was the first game produced by Bally in electronic format, but was never marketed as such.*

ABOVE LEFT Nitro Groundshaker; *typical Christensen art, including the usual obsession with buckles.*

ABOVE *Designer Greg Kmiec capitalizes on the worldwide fame of the Globetrotters.*

'remember' any targets that were hit, giving players more accurate scores. And digital games were also designed to play faster because the new electronics could keep up with even the fastest ball's scoring. Interestingly, the electronics inside pinball games can tally the ball's scoring instantly, just as pocket calculators add figures. Manufacturers learned that players enjoy hearing large bonuses being counted off 1,000 points at a time, as well as the ringing of

ABOVE *Inevitably, T.V. tie-ins became more and more common.*

BELOW RIGHT *Spelling B-A-L-L-Y on* Star Trek *increased the bonus.*

(1978), Gottlieb continued making mechanical games for the few players who felt more comfortable with the same style of pinball machines that they grew up with, although by now it was clear that electronic pinballs were the wave of the future.

Solid state technology also brought down production costs, allowing manufacturers to produce all pinballs as four-player games. Since score reels first appeared in the fifties, it had always been more expensive to build a multiple-player game than a single-player; in the 1970s, a four-player machine might cost $150 more than a two-player model, which in turn might cost $100 more than a single-player game, a substantial difference in those days. However, with solid state circuitry, the cost difference between a four-player and a single-player was

the bells when high scoring targets are hit, so pinball games are programmed to register points as quickly as possible but with enough bonus chimes to keep players happy.

In November of 1977, Bally unveiled *Eight Ball*, a machine that demonstrated just what was possible with the new solid-state technology. The playfield, designed by George Christian, was fairly ordinary. Artist Paul Faris based the pool-themed game's artwork on the popular *Happy Days* TV series. But this machine could do things no other pinball had done before because it had a memory! *Eight Ball* remembered what targets were hit on the first ball, and when a player began his second ball, those targets would already be lit. *Eight Ball* set a pinball production record, with 20,230 games built, a record that still stands today.

While Bally was producing *Eight Ball*, Gottlieb, Williams and Stern were turning out electronic pinballs of their own. Gottlieb's *Sinbad* (1977) featured four flippers lined up across the bottom of the playfield and was one of that company's most popular pinballs ever. While producing electronic pinballs like *Cleopatra* (1977) and *Joker Poker*

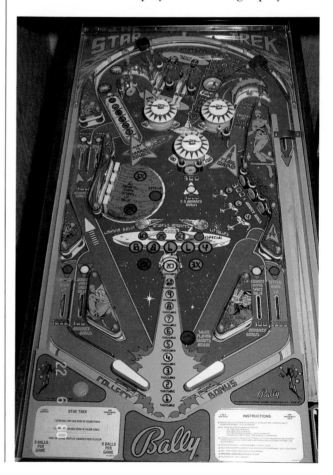

minimal, and with the greater flexibility of multiple-player machines, single-player pinballs disappeared, although Gottlieb experimented with *Asteroid Annie And The Aliens*, a single-player game in 1980, which proved to be a disaster. Bally went in the other direction with *The Six Million Dollar Man* (1978), a six-player electronic game. Inspired by Bally pinball chief Norman Clark, designed by Greg Kmiec and with artwork by Dave Christensen, it was based on the TV series of the same name. Although more than 10,000 of these games were built, players never really utilized the machine's six-player capability, which Clark later said was one of his biggest disappointments in pinball design.

By 1978, pinball manufacturers couldn't keep up with the demand for new games. The machines were everywhere, and as players' appetites for pinball increased, new manufacturers sprang up to fill the demand. A former Chicago Coin pinball designer

BELOW Four Million B.C. *was one of several multi-ball games that Bally brought out around the same time, among them* Wiggler, Capersville *and, of course,* Fireball.

RIGHT AND ABOVE RIGHT *The electronic* Sinbad *was also released in electromechanical form as* Eye of the Tiger.

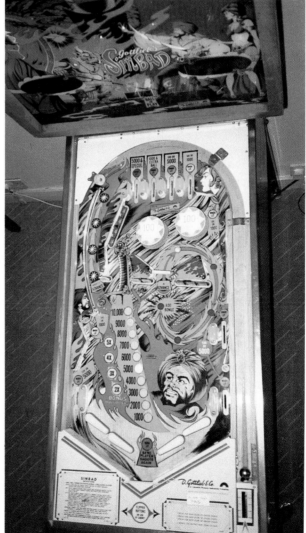

Wendell McAdams, decided to take advantage of the expanding market and produce a new style of pinball game. McAdams formed Game Plan, a company specializing in cocktail table-style machines. These sit-down pinballs were flat and inconspicuous, and ideally suited for locations that either couldn't fit a standard pinball or didn't want one because of the "gaudiness." Game Plan's first pinball, *Real*, was produced principally as a promotion for a cigarette company, while the next game, *Black Velvet*, advertised a brand of liquor. Game Plan produced several more cocktail pins before launching a line of conventional pinballs in 1979.

While the major pinball manufacturers steered clear of cocktail table-style pins, several companies decided that sit-down pinballs offered a relatively inexpensive way of breaking into the profitable pinball market. Valley (a pool table manufacturer), Venture (a video game company) and even Coffee-Mat (a company specializing in freshly brewed products) jumped on the pinball bandwagon, although all of them quickly left the pinball field after each producing only one game. Only Allied Leisure Industries and Game Plan experienced some degree of success with cocktail pinballs.

At about this same time, pinball manufacturers were also expanding into "wide body" games. About six inches wider than conventional machines, this large-size format had been pioneered by video giant Atari in 1977 with *The Atarians*. These wide games had a different feel to them which discouraged some players, but *The Atarians* was popular enough to keep Atari in the pinball market for three years, producing games including *Airborne Avenger* and *Space Riders* before releasing its last (and most popular) pinball – *Superman* – in 1979.

Bally, Williams, Gottlieb and Stern all produced their own wide-body machines between 1978 and 1981. Few of these games were successful, and once the novelty of the larger playfield wore off, players returned to the conventional sized machines, which had been in constant production alongside their larger brothers. Probably the most successful of these wide-body games was Bally's *Space Invaders Pinball* (1979),

ABOVE Voltan Escapes Cosmic Doom: *Comic book glamor from Dave Christensen.*

BELOW Space Invaders *was a wide-bodied game featuring infinity lighting effects.*

SUPERMAN

LEFT Superman *was designed by Steve Ritchie for Atari before he joined Williams.*

BELOW *Several visits were made by artists Dave Christensen and Paul Faris to the Playboy Mansion to ensure authenticity on this machine!*

James Bond (1980), while Stern produced *Ted Nugent* (1978) and *Muhammed Ali* (1979) among others.

One of the most popular celebrity tie-in pinballs was Bally's 1978 *Playboy*, designed by Jim Patla. *Playboy* may have seemed too sexist for some players, but a well-designed playfield had people lining up. Patla said *Playboy* was produced exactly as it was conceived on the drawing board, very unusual for a playfield layout. The sound was also an important part of the game's success, with wolf whistles and seductive music matching the theme perfectly. Paul Faris's artwork also drew players to the game. Faris, who incorporated depth and detail into his pinball art, pictured Hugh Hefner on the backglass, along with two of *Playboy* magazine's 1977 "playmates," All of *Playboy*'s familiar trademarks, including the famous bunny head, were pictured on the game. Hefner, reportedly a pinball player himself, even promoted the game in the pages of his magazine.

William O'Donnell, Jr., president of Bally's pinball division in the late 1970s, said in 1979 that

which featured strobing backbox lights and sound similar to its video counterpart. Designed by Jim Patla, *Space Invaders Pinball* had players lining up — many at 50 cents per game. Over 11,000 *Space Invaders Pinballs* were built to meet the demand for the game.

Celebrity pinball machines remained popular in the late 1970s. Continuing the trend started with *Wizard* and *Captain Fantastic*, Bally led the way with *Evel Knievel* (1977), *Star Trek* (1979), *Kiss* (1979), *Dolly Parton* (1979), *Rolling Stones* (1980) and others. Gottlieb also had its share of celebrity pinball games, including *Close Encounters Of The Third Kind* (1978), *Charlie's Angels* (1978), *Buck Rogers* (1979) and

not only did Bally look for stars to appear on their pinball games, but celebrities also approached Bally. Having a TV, movie or celebrity tie-in attracted players to the games, particularly when celebrities like Muhammed Ali participated in promotions and game giveaways.

Outer space still remained the most popular pinball theme. Gottlieb's *Countdown* (1978) pictured an astronaut watching a scantily clad space beauty from his ship, while Stern's *Stars* (1978) depicted various stellar scenes. Some games featured present-day activities in futuristic settings, such as Gottlieb's *Pinball Pool* (1978) which pictured a robot at a billiards table, Bally's *Future Spa* (1978), which illustrated the future of today's growing fitness trend and Williams' *Alien Poker* (1979), which had three

outer space aliens playing cards with the stakes being "control of the universe," according to the sales brochure.

Card game motifs were also popular on pinball machines. Bally's *Blackjack* (1978), Gottlieb's *Joker Poker* (1978), Williams' *Pokerino* (1978) and Stern's *Hot Hand* (1979) all featured either poker or black-jack themes. Another popular pinball subject is sport, with nearly every sport being featured on at least one game – baseball on Bally's *Grand Slam* (1982); football on Gottlieb's *Touchdown* (1984); basketball on Bally's *Harlem Globetrotters* (1979); hockey on Bally's *Power Play* (1978) and Game Plan's *Mike Bossy* (1982); soccer on Williams' *World Cup* (1978) and bowling on Bally's *Strikes And Spares* (1978) and Stern's *Memory Lane* (1978). Even skateboarding (Bally's *Skateball*, 1980) and roller skating (Gottlieb's *Roller Disco*, 1979) were immortalized on pinball machines.

Video games' influence on pinball themes was also growing. Bally, whose midway video division was enjoying a surge of popularity, brought out pinball games like *Space Invaders Pinball, Mr. And Mrs. Pac Man* (1982) and *Spy Hunter Pinball* (1984) to take advantage of the fame of their video counterparts.

FAR LEFT World Cup *was promoted in Europe by French soccer player Michel Platini.*

ABOVE LEFT Spectrum *speaks to the player giving clues as to how to score most effectively.*

ABOVE Pac-Man's *artwork was by Margaret Hudson. The game had a completely new-style cabinet.*

BELOW Future Spa *was a wide-bodied game featuring in-line drop targets, as seen on* Harlem Globetrotters.

Gottlieb's *Q*Bert's Quest* pinball (1982) tried to cash in on the success of the company's video hit, while Williams' *Defender* pinball incorporated elements of that company's video into a 1982 flipper game.

Artwork was also becoming more important on pinballs. Bally's *Lost World* (1978) is considered an artistic masterpiece with an almost three-dimensional effect. *Lost World* is one of artist Paul Faris' favorite designs, as the mythical hero in the artwork is actually a self-portrait of Faris, while his wife served as the model for the woman on the backglass. Faris said that heroic fantasies are his favorite style of art, and added that *Lost World's* backglass, which pictures him as a musclebound hero, is appropriate because Faris is himself a weightlifter. *Lost World's*

art was so popular with players that Faris used the characters again on Bally's *Paragon* (1979).

Drawing friends and relatives into backglass art is a common practice, particularly at Bally, where artists strive for realism in the drawings. According to several of Bally's staff artists, it's easier to create a drawing by working from a photograph of someone than doing a realistic drawing of an imaginary person. The youngsters pictured on the backglass of Bally's *BMX* (1982), for example, are actually friends and relatives of artist Greg Freres, while other Bally games such as *Mystic* (1979) and *Frontier* (1980) contain drawings of company employees.

In contrast to Bally's style of artwork, Gottlieb continued with the exaggerated, cartoonish style the company had been using for years. Gordon Morrison was the man responsible for much of Gottlieb's artwork at this time. Some of the games created under his influence are *Solar Ride* (1978) and *Genie* (1979).

In 1978, Williams hired a team of in-house artists rather than relying on outside efforts, and their first

Kmiec was probably the first to receive credit for his work on Bally's *Wizard* by having his name appear on the playfield, most designers remained anonymous throughout the seventies. Sharp-eyed players might notice the name "Kmiec" near the left flipper of Bally's *Xenon* (1979). Even more subtle was the way Bally's pinball designers often had their initials hidden in the playfield art. Gary Gayton's "G.G." is almost invisible near the top kickout saucer on *Star Trek*. And when pinball giant Harry Williams, the founder of Williams Electronics, began designing pinball games for Stern Electronics in the late seventies, it seemed only natural that his machines should bear the label "Designed By Harry Williams." Bally, Williams and Stern all allowed some degree of recognition for their designers on at least some of their games, although Gottlieb designers have remained anonymous.

Although movies had inspired many pinball themes, the reverse was the case in 1978 with the release of

TOP LEFT Flash *was Steve Ritchie's first electronic masterpiece for* Williams.

BELOW Xenon, *designed by Greg Kmiec, was the first game to speak with a woman's voice.*

LEFT *The exotic and attractive back glass of* Fathom, *released in 1981.*

creation was the art for the hit game *Flash*. With a lot of deep blue and black artwork, *Flash* was the first popular electronic pinball from Williams. The playfield was designed by Steve Ritchie, who started working on Atari pinballs before moving to Williams in 1978, and it featured an opening shot in which the ball emerged from the lower right corner of the playfield and traveled diagonally across the field to the upper left scoring area. With an exciting new sound system, *Flash* became one of the first pinball machines to feature background sound that increased in pitch and intensity the longer the ball was in play. It was the first pinball machine to grab players with a combination of artwork, sound and play action.

Pinball designers finally began receiving recognition for their work at about this time. Although Greg

GORGAR SPEAKS!

the movie *Tilt*. The film starred a young Brooke Shields as a teenaged pinball wizard who spent her life traveling and making money by winning pinball matches. She finally meets "The Whale" (Charles Durning), who challenges her to a game on his custom-designed *Cosmic Venus* pinball machine.

Tilt was an attempt by filmmaker Rudy Durand to take advantage of the country's pinball mania. Unfortunately, critics didn't like the movie at all — and neither did arcade owners. *Tilt* portrayed pinball as a form of gambling, which didn't help its image, already under attack in many local areas from people who equated the games with slot machines. *Tilt* faded quickly from view soon after its release, although the film still appears sometimes on syndicated television stations.

In 1979, another new pinball development appeared when Williams unveiled *Gorgar*, the world's first talking pingame. With a menacing voice to match the monster on the backglass, *Gorgar* taunted players with phrases like *Me, Gorgar, Beat Me* and *You Hurt Gorgar*. *Gorgar* even had a pounding heartbeat for a background sound. While Gorgar's voice wasn't always audible in noisy arcades, it demonstrated that

sound was becoming an increasingly important part of pinball. *Gorgar* had a better-than-average playfield layout, although its main claim to fame was its sound. Before long, talking pinballs became common. Most used digitized, mechanical-sounding voices because manufacturers felt that pinball machines should sound like machines. Usually the words or phrases that were spoken by the game were recorded and played back about 30 per cent slower for a robot-like sound. One notable exception was Bally's *Xenon* (1979), which used the voice of one of the company's female employees exactly as it was recorded. Although early talking pinball games attracted players, the novelty had worn off within a couple of years.

Williams' follow-up to *Gorgar* also became a big hit. *Firepower* was the first digital pinball to feature multiball play: pinball still had new ideas to explore. Created by Steve Ritchie, *Firepower* had a simple yet intriguing objective: spell out the word F-I-R-E-

ABOVE Gorgar: *the first talking pinball to be marketed.*

BELOW The Games *was brought out for the 1984 Olympics and was used in the World Pinball Championship that year.*

P-O-W-E-R, shoot the balls into the kickout saucers and get ready. Three balls rocket onto the playfield at once, creating a frustrating yet enjoyable game. *Firepower* also introduced "lane change," a feature that every pinball company eventually used. With lane change, players could shift the lit lanes on the playfield by pressing the flipper button, thus making it easier to complete high-scoring sequences. *Firepower* also featured speech and special lighting effects, and became the most successful Williams pinball game ever produced.

After *Firepower* appeared, multiball play became a regular feature on every manufacturer's games. Most machines featured simultaneous three-ball play, but others were designed for two-ball, four-ball, five-

BELOW Grand Lizard – *replete with Multi-ball, Magna-save and alpha-numeric displays.*

ABOVE Vector *had upper and lower playfields, four flippers, Multi-ball, and was a speaking machine. The theme was futuristic ice hockey.*

OPPOSITE, BELOW Jungle Lord *had Multi-ball, multi-level and Magna-save, and came with a choice of three cabinet colorways.*

OPPOSITE, ABOVE *After Williams'* High Speed, *lights appeared on the tops of the games. High-scoring players could enter their initials on* Gold Wings.

ball, and in one case, six-ball play! Multiball was actually an extension of the play appeal of most popular video games. On pre-*Firepower* pinball games, players focused all of their attention on the ball. Most videos, however, required players to divide their concentration among the action going on all over the screen. *Firepower*, like these videos, forced players to keep track of the entire playfield rather than simply focusing on one pinball.

But even multiball games weren't keeping players attracted to pinball. By 1980, video games like *Galaxian*, *Donkey Kong*, *Asteroids* and *Pac Man* had stolen the spotlight – and the players – from pinball. Pins were being replaced by the more compact and better-earning videos, especially in locations catering to younger players. Although the older "tavern crowd" still played pinball, the teenagers (who put most money into coin-op games) were getting hooked on videos.

Players hadn't given up on pinball entirely, though, especially when the next breakthrough game appeared in late 1980. Williams' *Black Knight* was considered the "ultimate" in pinball. Another Steve Ritchie creation, it was truly an electronic marvel, featuring a two-level playfield connected by ramps. The ball appeared on the upper level, complete with a full array of flippers and targets. The lower level had several new features including "magna-save" (electro-magnets hidden under the playfield in the outlanes and activated by an extra set of flipper buttons) and

"mystery score" (a timed bonus lane which scored a random value up to 99,000 points). As well as speaking phrases like *The Black Knight Will Slay You* and *Will You Challenge The Black Knight Again?*, the game also contained a doorbell-like device to draw attention to the game whenever a player received an extra ball or free game. On top of all this, *Black Knight* introduced "Bonus Ball": in a two-, three-, or four-player game, the highest-scoring player received 30–60 seconds of free play, with all three balls rolling around the double-level playfield at once. *Black Knight* was such a hit that many arcades charged 50 cents per game – with some *Black Knights* set higher for a three-ball game! The machine was such a success that some people predicted that single-level games would become extinct. Three more double-level multiball games followed from Williams – *Jungle Lord, Pharoah* and *Solar Fire* – but none managed to recapture the magic of *Black Knight*.

Only a few weeks after *Black Knight* appeared, Bally produced a double-level game of its own. *Flash Gordon* was designed by Claude Fernandez, who had only recently joined the Bally team after a stint at Williams. *Lightning* was Stern's first bi-level offering, created by Joseph Joos, Jr., who had designed

machines for Chicago Coin and Game Plan before settling at Stern. Gottlieb went in a different direction with its first double-level game, *Black Hole*. Instead of adding a second level on top of the playfield area, *Black Hole* featured an additional play area below the main field and visible through a transparent panel in the center of the main playfield. With its multi-level play, speech and a rotating wheel behind the backglass, *Black Hole* was popular with players. Gottlieb's next pinball went a step further; *Haunted House* was the first triple-level game, with extra playfields both above and below the main playboard to simulate the three floors of a house. The spooky organ music added to the effect, but although both *Black Hole* and *Haunted House* were successful, they weren't enough to rescue pinball from its slide in popularity.

To compete with the increasing popularity of video games, innovative new design ideas were introduced. Stern unveiled *Orbitor 1* in 1982, with a moonlike cratered landscape instead of a smooth playfield. Gottlieb's *Krull* pinball (1983) was another triple-level game, but with a new twist – the transparent cover over the lowest level was actually a reducing

ABOVE Haunted House *boasted not only playfields on three levels and eight flippers, but also a stirring rendition of Bach's Toccata and Fugue.*

RIGHT *Granny and the Gators combined video and pinball, on the premise that if you can't beat 'em, join 'em.*

1934. Although several new pinball games were on the drawing board at the time, Stern's two pinball designers, Joseph Joos, Jr. and Brian Poklacki, were assigned to the company's video division, and except for a single 1984 prototype pinball called *Lazerlord*, Stern was out of the pinball business forever.

Other pinball manufacturers had left the business even earlier than Stern. Allied Leisure Industries closed its doors in 1980 when the company was sold. And Atari left the field in 1979 to concentrate on its

glass, making the pinballs appear as tiny ball-bearings being hit by miniature flippers. Williams experimented with *Varkon*, a pinball in an upright video cabinet which used joysticks rather than buttons to control the flippers, in 1983. Williams also produced *Joust* (1983), a head-to-head style pinball in the tradition of Gottlieb's 1971 *Challenger* pinball.

Some pinball manufacturers even followed the old adage, "If you can't beat 'em, join 'em" and built combination pinball/video games. Gottlieb's *Caveman* (1982) had a standard-size pinball playfield with a video game screen mounted in the center, controlled by a joystick on the front of the cabinet. Bally produced *Baby Pac Man* (1982) and *Granny And The Gators* (1983) both featuring scaled-down pinball games in upright video game cabinets, with a video screen mounted vertically above the playfield. None of these unusual games left a permanent impression on players, though.

Despite all these innovations, pinball was hard hit by the popularity of video games. The pinball industry suffered a major loss in 1982 when Stern Electronics shut down its pinball division, ending a pinball tradition that started with Chicago Coin in

video game production. By the end of 1982, many industry "experts" were predicting the permanent demise of pinball. "Pinball was dead," they said, adding that the only places were pinball machines would be found in two or three years would be museums.

For a while, these prophecies seemed accurate. Most of the pinball manufacturers had drastically cut the size of their design staffs. Fewer new models appeared, and most of those that were produced had very limited production runs. Games like Williams' *Cosmic Gunfight* (1983) and *Warlok* (1983), Bally's *BMX* (1982) and *Gold Ball* (1983) and Gottlieb's *Punk* (1983) and *Striker* (1983) were all produced in such low quantities that they remain virtually unknown to players.

To stay in production, pinball manufacturers were forced to cut back on production costs. Double-level games were out, and multiball machines became scarce as manufacturers saved on the added cost of

the multiball mechanism. Talking games became less common (the speech chips cost about $50–$75, and elaborate new playfield features were introduced sparingly as designers concentrated more on the basics.

Nearly every electronic pinball produced until this time had been a four-player game. To reduce production costs, Bally's *Grand Slam* (1983) and Williams' *Defender* (1983) and *Time Fantasy* (1983) were produced as two-player models. Bally even went a step further when it tried to reintroduce the add-a-ball concept on a single-player game. Bally's Norman Clark explained it this way: "When we made *Speakeasy* (1982), the intention was to bring out an add-a-ball, which had kind of been buried. The thought was, 'There are a lot of players who like to play add-a-balls.' I myself liked add-a-ball. So we decided to make an add-a-ball. We made a single-player add-a-ball, and it turned out that Germany in particular said 'We won't take a single-player, it has to be a multi-player.' So we went on and developed it

ABOVE BMX *featured extra buttons which allowed the player a limited number of attempts to close the exit lanes. The game was later issued, with modifications, as* Hard Body.

BELOW Lightning *was one of the last designs from Stern before they bowed out of the Pinball business.*

87

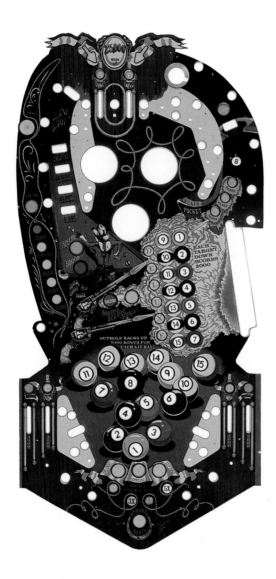

LEFT *The playfield of* Eight Ball deLuxe, *before the components are added.*

RIGHT Road Kings *was used for the 1987 Pinball World Championship.*

popular mechanical pinballs of the 1970s; *Orbit* (1972) became *Super Orbit* (1983), *Royal Flush* (1976) became *Royal Flush Deluxe* (1983), *Jacks Open* (1977) became *Jacks To Open* (1984) and *El Dorado* (1975) became *El Dorado And The City Of Gold* (1984). And Game Plan unveiled *Sharpshooter II* (1984), with a playfield identical to its 1979 *Sharpshooter* game but with new sounds and artwork.

Williams used a slightly different approach, updating popular electronic games of only a few years earlier by rearranging or adding several targets, flippers, etc. *Blackout* (1980) was modified to become *Warlok* (1983), *Alien Poker* (1980) underwent minor changes and was reissued as *Laser Cue* (1984) and the wide body game *Laser Ball* (1979) was reworked into standard size pinball machine as *Starlight* (1984).

The most eagerly awaited remake, though, was Bally's 1985 electronic reissue of its classical mechanical *Fireball* machine. After numerous requests from players and collectors, Bally finally decided the time was right to produce an electronic version of its 1972 hit. Except for replacing the old-style small "zipper flippers" with standard size flippers, *Fireball Classic* was an exact duplicate of the original game. When the machine was being re-engineered, though, designer George Christian found that the stronger thumper bumpers used on today's faster electronic games were putting too much force on the ball, and damaging several playfield parts, so weaker bumpers were used, leading some players to believe that the machine wasn't working properly. Christian also added a bonus sytem and bonus multiplier, features which the original *Fireball* didn't have, but which had become standard on machines by the 1980s. *Fireball Classic* played very much like Ted Zale's original design. It is a pity that as pinball

into a two-player. The game went over to Monte Carlo at a show and the consensus of opinion was, 'We don't want a two-player, we want a four-player.' So the single-player add-a-ball eventually became a four-player. We did put out some two-players, but it turned into a four-player game. And that took care of us trying to make single-players once again. Or add-a-balls, for that matter."

Pinball remakes became another method for manufacturers to keep production costs low. Gottlieb produced electronic versions of several of its more

attract players. *Eight Ball Deluxe* was so popular, in fact, that Bally produced a "Limited Edition" of the game the following year to fill the demand. Even today, the game still attracts players.

Bally's *Centaur* (1981) was another pinball game that was much more popular than anyone would have expected. The artwork, done almost entirely in black and white (with a touch of red) pictured a half-human motorcycle gang. Artist Paul Faris was looking for something eye-catching to go along with designer Jim

machines had become more sophisticated in design, players were unimpressed with this modern version.

There were some bright spots for pinball at this time, though. Bally's *Eight Ball Deluxe* (1982) was one of them. Designer George Christian created this "sequel" to his popular 1977 *Eight Ball* game (although *Eight Ball Deluxe* had a completely original design with a country/western tavern theme). *Eight Ball Deluxe* became the "sleeper" pinball hit of 1982, proving much more popular with players than Bally had ever expected it to be. *Eight Ball Deluxe* had no flashy gimmicks or unusual features, but was simply a basic, easy-to-understand game with a wide open playfield. The game's speech was also a plus, with phrases like *Quit Talking And Start Chalking* to

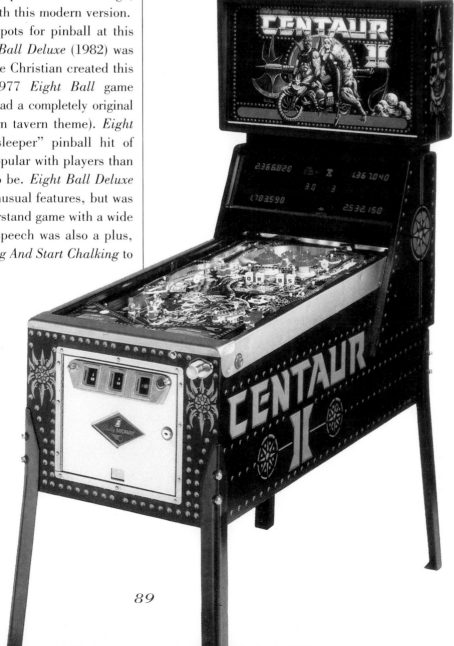

RIGHT Centaur II; *the original Centaur had employed video black-and-white imagery; ironically, videos were by now using full color, so the designers had to decide whether or not to move with the times once again – by "reverting" to color!*

LEFT *By the time* Arena *was produced in 1987, Gottlieb had moved away from the traditional screening method of producing the back glass. They now use a photographic laminating process frowned upon by the purists.*

ABOVE *On* Escape From the Lost World *Bally applied additional artwork to the glass over the playfield.*

OPPOSITE *Fire was a speaking game designed by Mark Ritchie for Williams; the voice pleads "Save my Baby!" A "Champagne" edition was also produced, with an oak cabinet and gold fittings.*

Patla's playfield layout, and he found it. Patla created *Centaur* to pay tribute to Bally's 1956 multiball game *Balls-A-Poppin'*. Like *Balls-A-Poppin'*, players could get up to six balls in play at once on *Centaur*, providing some frenzied action *Centaur's* multiball technique was unusual, though, because the balls were launched from a hidden flap in the plunger lane, sometimes catching players off guard. Only 3,700 *Centaurs* were produced, but like *Eight Ball Deluxe*, *Centaur* was such an overwhelming success that the game went back into production in 1983 under the name Centaur II. Centaur was the last pinball designed by Patla, now the head of Bally's pinball design department, and is still his favorite game.

Later, in 1984, disaster seemed poised to strike the pinball industry. Columbia Pictures, which owned Gottlieb, decided that amusement games weren't profitable any more and closed the historic company, once the unquestioned leader of the pinball industry. Gilbert Pollack, a Gottlieb employee, decided to take a major gamble. He gathered a small group of investors, bought all the company's pinball assets, and resurrected the Gottlieb name on the new Premier pinball line. He even kept most of the Gottlieb design staff. Although disaster was averted and the Gottlieb pinball tradition continued uninterrupted, it had seemed for a while that one of the world's pinball giants would be lost.

At about the same time, rumors had been circulating that Williams was in serious financial trouble and might have to close its doors unless it came up with a hit game immediately. Luckily, that's just what happened. Williams' *Space Shuttle* was unveiled in November, 1984 at the industry's annual trade show, and took everyone by storm. *Space Shuttle* had everything — excellent sound, terrific artwork, special effects — but most importantly, a great playfield layout designed by Barry Oursler. Williams spared no expense putting the game together, even including a miniature space shuttle model on the playfield. There

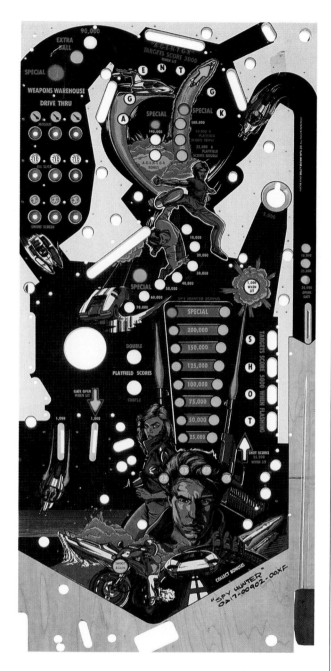

was the price – several hundred dollars less than most other manufacturers' games. But although the machine played very fast, it never fared well and Wico never made another pinball game.

The other new pinball manufacturer, Pinstar, unveiled *Gamatron* at the same trade show. *Gamatron* was not a conventional pinball, but rather a conversion kit. About half the price of a new pinball machine, *Gamatron* was basically a complete pinball playfield, backglass and circuit board which could be installed into an older pinball cabinet. *Gamatron's* playfield was actually an updated version of Stern's *Flight 2000* pinball (1980), designed by Harry Williams. Most players couldn't tell the difference between *Gamatron* and other new machines, and the conversion idea never caught on. *Gamatron* was Pinstar's only pinball game.

Early in 1985, Gottlieb/Premier unveiled *Chicago Cubs Triple Play*, which introduced "alphanumerics" to pinball. The digital scoring readouts had been modified to spell out words and messages, directing players to specific playfield targets and allowing the top scorers to enter their initials in the game's electronics. Although the game was only a moderate success, the alphanumerics were an instant hit.

In the fall of 1985, Williams once again introduced the pinball hit of the year – *Comet*, which featured an amusement park theme and a long transparent ramp in the center of the playfield. *Comet* also featured the first one million point shot. Though most players didn't recognize them, the playfield was strewn with hidden references to people who had had a hand in putting the game together. Company vice president Joseph Dillon is pictured as "Dare Dillon." Playfield designer Barry Oursler is alluded to in "Barry's

were two ramps on the game leading to multiball play, with kickout saucers, drop targets, lane change and a ball-return gate completing the design. *Space Shuttle* was the most popular game – pinball or video – at that show.

At the same show, two new pinball manufacturers came on the scene. Wico, a company which for years had supplied spare parts for pinballs, presented *Af-Tor*. The machine was the first wide body game produced for several years, and featured an unusual cabinet design. *Af-Tor's* biggest selling point, though,

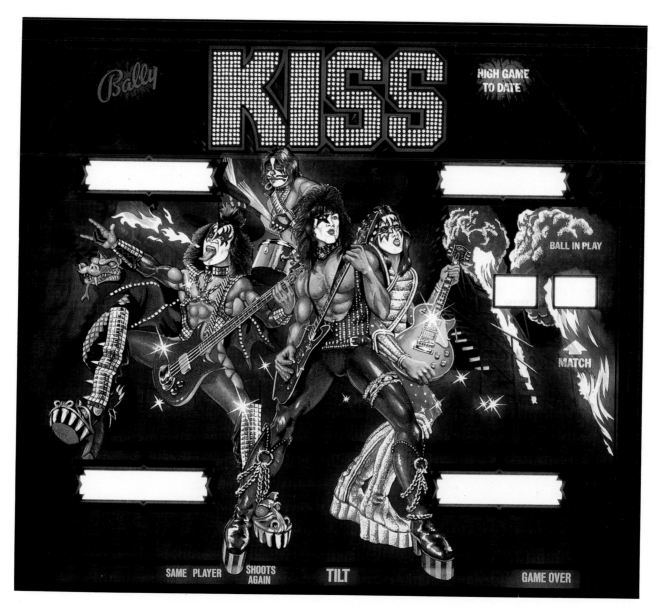

Game Gallery," while "Ken's Vending" refers to engineering chief Ken Fedesna. Others who had contributed to *Comet*'s development were immortalized in other ways. When the ramp to the one million point shot is lit, design chief Steve Kordek's voice chants *A Million!* over and over. And when *Comet*'s drop target is hit, revealing a hidden recessed target, the player has only a few seconds to make the shot while Oursler's voice tauntingly says, *Hey, Turkey! C'mon, Hit Me!*

Comet was conceived with an amusement park theme right from the start. "*Comet* came about with the suggestion, the idea of a theme," recalled Kordek. "Somebody suggested 'Let's talk about an amuse-ment park theme.' Well, an amusement park theme sounds very good until you decide 'What are you going to do with an amusement park theme?' Then you start thinking back, as we have on *Comet* – a roller coaster, we have the Dunk The Dummy, we have the love boat area, we have the ducks, we have the rabbits that you're shooting for, we have the choo-choo train that runs around. Well, this all develops as you go along."

Game themes are often more flexible, though. Bally's *Harlem Globetrotters* pinball (1979) was originally called *Red Baron*, but was renamed when Bally decided to feature the well-known basketball team on a game. A similar situation arose in 1984,

when an auto racing-themed pinball design was changed to *Spy Hunter Pinball* after Bally's marketing department determined that the popular *Spy Hunter* video game's name would draw players.

At about the same time that *Comet* appeared, a new manufacturer, Grand Products, introduced its first (and only) pinball, which like Pinstar's *Gamatron*, was marketed as a conversion kit. Grand Products' *Bullseye 301* had a fairly ordinary playfield, but featured a new method of scoring. Designed around a darts theme, the player started with a score of 301 at the beginning of each game. The targets scattered

LEFT Pinbot *was the tournament game for the Pinball Expo' of 1986; its open playfield made for frenetic action and demanded skillful ramp and plunger shots.*

around the playfield then subtracted points, a few at a time, until the player reached zero, the same scoring method used in the darts game of 301. Unfortunately, conversion pinballs were still not very popular, and the scoring confused many players who were not familiar with darts, so the game was not a great success.

Gottlieb/Premier explored another dimension in pinball art early in 1986 with *Raven*. For the first time, a photograph was used on the backglass rather than hand-drawn artwork. *Raven* was a "female Rambo" portrayed by Susie Jablonski, a Chicago-area resident employed by a local health and fitness club. *Raven* and subsequent Gottlieb/Premier photo backglasses were shot on location for authenticity, rather than being staged in a photographer's studio. Bally also tried a photo backglass on *Hardbody* (1987), featuring woman bodybuilder Rachel MacLish. The playfield art remained hand-drawn on all of these games, making for an attractive mix of art and photography.

Gottlieb/Premier's *Monte Carlo* (1987) had an interesting photo backglass to complement the game's casino theme. The photo was shot in Chicago's Gaslight Club, and pictured Alvin Gottlieb (son of company founder David Gottlieb) wearing a lavender tuxedo, and Gilbert Pollack, Gottlieb/Premier president, along with several professional models. *Monte Carlo's* playfield featured a roulette wheel spinner to award bonus points, as well as the first ten million point shot in pinball.

The photo backglass on Gottlieb/Premier's *Genesis* (1986) is also interesting because it pictures a mad scientist and his assistants in their laboratory, which is actually a wall covered with pinball parts and spray-painted black. And although the outfit worn by the girl in the photo looks real, it was actually retouched when it was determined that the dress she had posed in for the photo might be too revealing.

Williams produced another big pinball hit early in 1986 with *High Speed*. This Steve Ritchie game fea-

ABOVE Party Animal *offered the player a choice of soundtracks to* *select from the miniature jukebox, as he hit appropriate targets.*

tured a police chase theme with a flashing red light atop the machine. With green-, yellow- and red-light targets on the playfield, *High Speed* included an open-ended ramp, kickback lane and alphanumerics. Another innovation was the "jackpot bonus": if a player makes the ramp shot during multiball play, a jackpot bonus of up to two million points is awarded. The game's motif, a car chase on the Santa Monica freeway, was developed after Ritchie himself was involved in a high-speed chase on that highway. Like many of Ritchie's earlier games, *High Speed* was easy to understand (complete the traffic light sequence then shoot for the ramp) but difficult to master.

High Speed was also the first pinball to include automatic replay percentaging. Until now, the score needed for a free game (say, one million points) would be preset on the machine. With *High Speed*, the free game score would be automatically shifted either higher or lower, depending on how many free games had been awarded to players. So if *High Speed* was being played somewhere with many skilled players, the machine would automatically raise the score needed for a free game, just as the score would be lowered if most players did poorly. Everyone seemed to like *High Speed*, including video-game players who hadn't touched a pinball machine in years. If an arcade had only one pinball, this would be it.

LEFT *A game with a wealth of player options, as can be seen from the playfield; photographic/laminate process for the artwork.*

BELOW LEFT Hollywood Heat obviously owes much to "Miami Vice".

While *High Speed* was the hottest game around, other machines were also attracting attention from players who had just discovered the joy of pinball for the first time. Gottlieb/Premier's *Hollywood Heat* had a theme reminiscent of television's *Miami Vice* and featured another photo backglass (reportedly *Miami Vice's* Don Johnson had talked to Gottlieb/Premier about appearing on the game, although a final agreement was never worked out). Over at Bally, new game ideas were being explored. Designer Greg Kmiec's *City Slicker* pinball featured a remote-control flipper button at the end of a long cable attached to the game. This button operated a strategically placed flipper in the center of the playfield, and if two or more people were playing, this extra flipper could be used to divert a competing player's ball away from high scoring targets. Unfortunately, this concept never caught on, and the few *City Slickers* which were produced were built without this remote control feature.

All the pinball manufacturers enjoyed a good year in 1987, with Williams leading the way with its hit game *Pinbot*. *Pinbot*, another Barry Oursler design, featured disappearing targets. When a target sequence is completed, the entire row of targets drops below the playfield level, revealing two kickout saucers which lock up balls for multiball play. Another talking game, *Pinbot* also had a transparent mini-level playfield suspended over the main play area.

Bally's *Strange Science* (1986) and *Party Animal* (1987), along with Gottlieb/Premier's *Victory* (1987) were also enjoyed by players. And video-game manufacturer Data East unveiled its first pinball, *Laser War*, in 1987 and received an enthusiastic response from players.

The pinball obituaries which had been written only three or four years ago were forgotten, and pinball was back in the spotlight once again. As a new generation of players gets its first taste of pinball, it looks as if the silverball will be bouncing around for some time to come.

BELOW Raven *cashed in on "Rambo" –
with a few modifications.*

PINBALL AT HOME

*H*aving succumbed to the lure of the silverball, what do you do? There is only one effective cure known for Silverballmania: make friends with a pinball machine. And the best way to do that is to invite it into your home. Before you can have a pinball machine at home there is some preparation to be done . . . namely placating the wife, girlfriend, partner. That done, you are ready to start looking for your new friend!

■ *WHERE DO YOU START?*   There are several possibilities: Yellow Pages under *Amusement Places* or *Amusement Devices (Coin Operated)*, the "For Sale" advertisements in the local "trader" papers and the collectors' publications. There is another option for those with about $2,500 (plus tax) to spend, and that is to go to an Amusement Machine Distributor and buy a new machine. However, it is not at all necessary to spend that much money: for a lot less you can still buy a machine that is very good value. Besides, you may prefer a pinball with some history/ nostalgia to it.

The first rule when buying your machine is to play the game, literally. This is important for two reasons: (1) to make sure it works; (2) to make sure you enjoy the game on offer. Like all rules, there is an exception. This is when the game is on offer under circumstances where it is not possible to plug it in, turn it on and let your fingers dance on those magic flipper buttons. In this situation it would be judicious to assume that the game is in less than perfect working order and to ensure that this is reflected in the finally agreed buying price.

■ *HOW MUCH SHOULD YOU PAY?*   Prices vary dramatically depending on where you buy and under what circumstances. If you are buying from an "Amusement Operator" you would be wise to remember that they are running a business. Nevertheless, they may still welcome the opportunity to pass on a machine that has out-lived its usefulness to

them. This does not mean that their opening price will be the lowest selling price! Like anything else it pays to shop around. This is particularly true of pinballs.

What are the other options? The "For Sale" columns are for the adventurous. These provide your best chance of picking up a bargain, though you must be prepared to haggle. For various reasons – original high price, sentiment, the belief that what is being offered is a rare collectors' item – an outrageously high price may be demanded. This is, in short, a source with a wide price range. But let me burst the bubble of a common misconception: there are no rare pintables worth extraordinarily high prices, with one possible exception – *Fireball* (Bally 1972). This historic game is often particularly sought after and, a good working example can change hands for up to $1,000. See Chapter 7 (Dave Christensen's Art), if you're wondering why. But, *Fireball* excepted, there are neverthe-

BELOW *Devil's Dare, a wide-bodied game up for auction, in this case at the annual UK convention.* **RIGHT** *The owner of this machine has over 90 others! So beware – if you're hooked, you stay hooked. Fathom is a pretty multi-ball game with two bonus systems. It's a speaking machine with the voice of a deep-sea diver.*

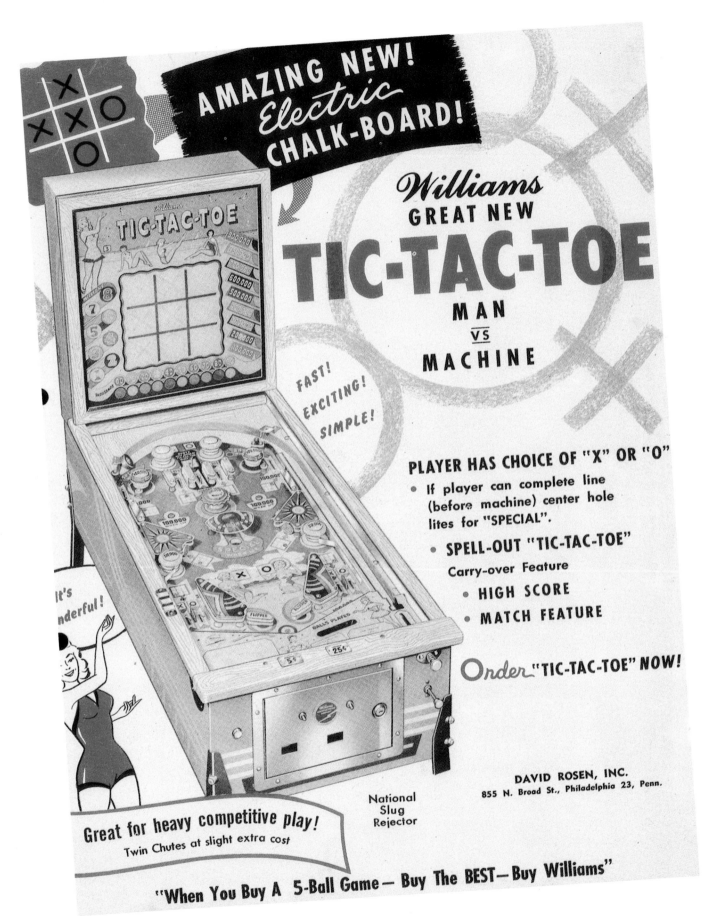

OPPOSITE *You may wish to collect machines with similar themes; this Williams game, like Happy Days illustrated on page 40, OXO on page 102, and X's and O's on page 107, is based on tic-tac-toe.*

ABOVE *This postcard was sent to the author by Bally to promote their new game Goldball.*

less some games that are more desirable than others; for this reason, though they may cost little more than their less prized relations, they will be easier to sell. Don't forget, beauty is in the eye – or rather the flipper fingers – of the player. So, while you should be guided by the advice of a knowledgeable friend, the ultimate decision must be yours.

Lastly, you can buy your pintable through one of the collectors' magazines. This method will give you the best opportunity to buy a good machine at a fair price. Here, in the experts' market place, the regular users of this means of sale or purchase will know the fair price of the game. What is more important, when you are offered a "working machine" it is likely to be fully working rather than something needing "minor" attention which you might find through other sources.

You should expect to pay between $200–$350 for an electromechanical game in good working condition. This price relates to games made in the 1960s and 1970s.

■ *ELECTRONIC GAMES* Toward the end of the 1970s pinball machines began to exploit the latest technology, i.e., the microchip. Electronic games have a significant advantage over the previous generation of games. They are, for example, more reliable. On the other hand when they do go wrong they may cost more to repair. However, when repairs are necessary, if you do not intend to do your own repairs and maintenance, and do not know a friendly pinball mechanic, you will be able to remove the faulty component and send it away for attention. It is easy to detect what

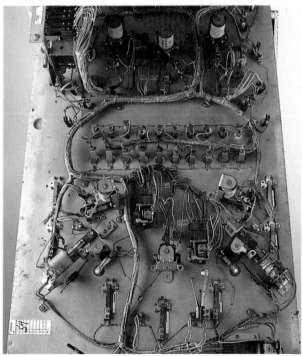

has gone wrong because electronic games have a built-in feature known as "self-test." This is activated by a switch found inside the front door, which enables you to sequence through the lights, solenoids and switches to identify which, if any, are not functioning correctly.

As the technology applied to pinball machines becomes more sophisticated, more and more automatic test facilities are being programmed into the games. This has now got to the point where, when you switch on the machine, the windows that during play show the scores, will now display the identity of any faulty parts, thus making it very easy for the least technically minded of us to replace bad parts with operational ones so that once again the game functions one hundred per cent.

If, after the machine has told you which features are non-operational you choose to start a game . . . no the machine does not send 50,000 volts zooming up your arms as soon as you touch the flipper buttons! Instead it reprograms the game to bypass those non-working features so that you get the best game possible under the circumstances.

So how much is one of these marvels of modern technology going to set you back? The answer is "Not as much as you might imagine." Remember that when such machines come onto the market they have already earned their keep. Expect to pay between $250 and $800 for a game over seven years old. Before you complete the deal, ask for the paperwork for the machine. For electromechanical games this will usually be a mere schematic. For an electronic game, in addition to the schematic, the manual will include setting-up instructions, game-setting instructions, troubleshooting tips and other useful information.

ABOVE *The inside of* Magic City; *a daunting sight, and one argument for collecting electronic machines which are more up-to-date, because diagnosis of* problems *is much easier and separate components can be replaced or sent away for repair.* TOP *The tic-tac-toe theme continues with* OXO (1974); *and* in the eighties, Bally produced X's & O's (page 107). ABOVE RIGHT *A real talking point in any collection, a four-player sit-down electronic game. The* playfield revolves so that the flippers come to each player in turn.

GETTING YOUR GAME INDOORS

Having acquired your game you will need to get it home. If you are fortunate it will be delivered by the seller, who will, no doubt, stick around and help you to get the machine up and running. For this reason it is worth spending a bit more to cover delivery.

If delivery is not part of the deal, do not despair. You will find it very helpful if you can be around while your purchase is being dismantled. Watch the dismantling process – this will help with the re-assembly. Whether you have bought an electro-mechanical game or an electronic one the general procedure is the same. Think of the game as two boxes, the larger is the "body" and the smaller is the "head." Add to these four legs and you have completed the persona of your new friend.

To take the machine apart (the process for assembly is the same in reverse) first remove the silver balls and any loose items inside the body. These will include the cash box and any debris and spare parts that may be around. Then remove the plugs from the head. In the case of electronic games you will need to release the braided ground wire that is attached by a screw or wing-nut. Do this only after all the plugs have been removed. With Stern games it is also necessary to remove the plugs from the power supply board and speaker inside the body before removing the head.

Then undo the bolts that couple the head to the body. Next, remove the back legs and stand the machine on its "legless" end so that the coin slots point to the sky. Now remove the front legs and the process is complete.

When re-assembling your machine the sequence is: front legs on, followed by the back legs; then remember to remove the mains lead from the body before bolting on the head. (There is usually a channel cut in the neck of the body for the lead to sit in.) Once the head is on you are ready to replace the

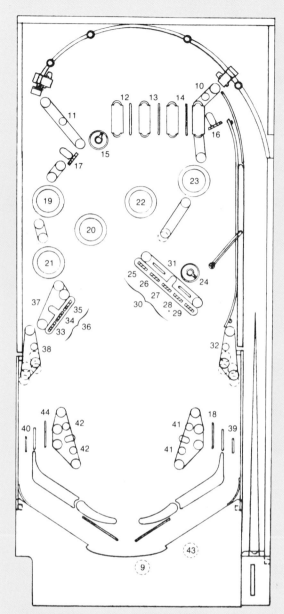

No.	Function	No.	Function
1	Plumb Bob Tilt	23	Right Jet Bumper
2	Ball Roll Tilt	24	Right Eject
3	Credit Button	25	5-Bank Drop Target #1 (Top)
4	Right Open Switch	26	5-Bank Drop Target #2
5	Center Coin Switch	27	5-Bank Drop Target #3
6	Left Coin Switch	28	5-Bank Drop Target #4
7	Slam Tilt	29	5-Bank Drop Target #5 (Bottom)
8	High Score Reset	30	5-Bank Drop Target Series
9	Outhole	31	5-Bank Standup
10	Upper Right Standup	32	Right Standup
11	Upper Left Standup	33	3-Bank Drop Target Left
12	"A" Rollover	34	3-Bank Drop Target Center
13	"B" Rollover	35	3-Bank Drop Target Right
14	"C" Rollover	36	3-Bank Drop Target Series
15	Top Eject Hole	37	3-Bank Standup
16	Bulls'-Eye Target	38	Left Standup
17	Left Target	39	Right Outside Rollover
18	Right Inside Rollover	40	Left Outside Rollover
19	Left Top Jet Bumper	41	Right Kicker
20	Left Center Jet Bumper	42	Left Kicker
21	Left Bottom Jet Bumper	43	Playfield Tilt
22	Right Center Jet Bumper	44	Left Inside Rollover

plugs. With electronic games it is important that you refix the ground strap before connecting any of the plugs: the purpose of this is to protect the microchips from any static discharge.

Do not be intimidated by what seems at first to be a confusing complex of plugs. Two things that will help you to ensure the correct male and female parts are mated. First, the length of the leads will suggest where the plug should go. The longer the lead, the further the socket. Second, manufacturers try to ensure that each plug and socket pair are unique. It should not be necessary, therefore, to use even the slightest amount of force to mate the plug and socket.

Now your game is set up what can you do to improve it?

RESTORING YOUR PINBALL MACHINE

(This section is not intended as a technical guide to the repair of pingames. But it does give some tips to help the non-technical person to keep a game in tip-top condition.)

At this stage, even with a game bought "in working order," you can raise the reliability and enjoyment level of your machine by various means:

(1) Remove the playfield glass, raise the playfield and pick up any loose items that look as if they should be part of the machine, then, using a vacuum cleaner with a small nozzle, remove dust, broken glass, matchsticks and any other gunk in the body.

While you are delving into the depths of your electromechanical friend it is a good idea to check that the fuses are the correct value. On newer machines the fuses may not be in the body, in which case you will find them in the head. It is particularly important that fuses of the correct value are used in electronic machines as too high a value can result in costly repairs!

(2) Next, lower the playfield and remove all light-shield plastics, posts (and playfield rubbers) and bulbs. Then, with any drop targets in the "down" position, you are ready to clean the playfield.

Be careful with your choice of cleaning solution as some chemicals may remove the playfield design. Don't use anything too abrasive.

What you need is a cleaner that will remove the accumulation of grime and polish, etc, and restore the brightness of the paint without damaging the paintwork. If in doubt, experiment on a part of the playfield that is not in prominent view or stick to soap and water.

LEFT *The fighting couples outside the boxing ring light up as the score climbs on* Knock Out; *you may be seduced into collecting older machines by the charming period feel of the artwork.*

RIGHT X's & O's; *as the publicity proclaims, "An exciting new contribution to the tic-tac-toe legacy."*

Having cleaned the playfield the next thing to do is seal it and create a smooth surface for the silver-ball to glide over. I have been advised to use a clear polyurethene varnish at this stage. This seems a bit radical, however, and I would recommend the traditional method of using a good quality silicon or wax polish.

Do not use a spray polish as you can't control where it goes, and you don't want to coat the electrical contacts and cause operating problems. After buffing up the playfield replace the bulbs, making sure they are all working. While you're doing this you might want to remove the backglass, clean the reverse of it very gently and check the bulbs behind it, replacing any faulty ones.

Now that all the bulbs are brightly lit you are ready to gently clean the playfield parts that you removed earlier. Usually soapy water or a foaming cleanser are the most effective. Be gentle when cleaning any parts, such as playfield plastics, that have unique artwork on them, because any damage will be difficult to repair or replace. Beware of adding to any damage caused by wear and tear by over-enthusiastic cleaning.

After cleaning and replacing the playfield parts, including the replacement of used playfield rubbers with new ones (typically an annual event for machines in home use), clean and polish the playfield glass, inside and out, and the outside of the backglass. Your pintable should now be fresh and sparkling and ready to reward you with many fast and exciting games.

MAINTAINING YOUR PINBALL MACHINE

Having carried out the procedures mentioned above, the amount of maintenance work required should be minimal: simply clean and polish all glass and wax and polish the playfield now and then.

The parts you will need for maintenance, such as bulbs and rubber parts, will be available from your Amusement Machine Distributor. Here, too, you can buy specialist cleaning and polishing materials for pintables, although the common domestic equivalent meets the needs of most people.

Alternatively, your local pinball palace might be a good place to ask for parts, advice and assistance. You never know unless you try. If you're enthusiastic about something that keeps a man employed, he just might help you.

HAPPY FLIPPING !

Introducing... XS & OS T.M.

SINCE THE DAWN OF SPARE TIME...
man has instinctively looked to tic-tac-toe as an essential source of light hearted merriment offering escape from the toils of daily life.

Through the ages, this simplistically charming game has brought about major changes in the social and political structure of American frivolity. Historians agree that the cultural contributions provided by tic-tac-toe surpass those of charades, bingo and even musical chairs.

Today, public demand for participation in the bountiful whimsies of this timeless game has reached tumultuous proportions with the advent of BALLY MIDWAY's most exciting new contribution to the tic-tac-toe legacy.

Bally MIDWAY T.M.

PINBALL EPHEMERA

A major attraction to coin-op collectables stems from nostalgia, our fond memories of ideas and events which are no longer present. We like to hold on to examples of Americana which reflect past moments of glory, famous people and the "good old days." *Apollo* serves as a reminder of the United States' pioneering achievements in technology and space travel.

Themes in pinball based upon contemporary situations or celebrities are to be found throughout its fifty years of commercial existence. A game that was named after a popular person, either real or fictitious (*Evel Knievel*, Bally 1977; *Daisy Mae*, Gottlieb 1954), or even an imaginary rabbit (*Harvey*, Williams 1951) stands out from the myriad of other games because it relates to a character we feel we know. The same principle applies to pinballs that mirror well-known points in US history (*Spirit Of '76*, Gottlieb 1976;

and three versions of *Gold Rush:* Rock-Ola 1935, Bally 1966 and Williams 1971). Remember that games which follow such themes have more collector value.

Timeliness of a machine's release to production and distribution was essential to its full impact on the public consciousness. If a pinball hit the streets within six months of an event or a celebrity's peak of popularity, it was more likely to enjoy commercial success. Some efforts were not very timely! Gottlieb's *Four Square* (1971) was supposed to show influences of the psychedelic era, which actually was emerging as early as 1967. Fortunately, the game stood up well on the merits of its playability. When the contemporary theme was used for a pinball game, it was sometimes phased into a design which was already under development. In such cases, aspects of the theme were attached with less regard for the need of the game's play scheme to reflect them.

The add-a-ball version of Apollo *was called* Lift Off; Apollo *featured a bagatelle in the "head".*

OPPOSITE *The grid on the* Hot Line *playfield spelled out* H-O-T-L-I-N-E; *quite a feat by designer Steve Kordek, without the aid of microchips.*

■ *SPACE WAS THE PLACE IN 1967* *Apollo* was released in June of 1967, at the time when public consciousness of space travel was riding high. Earlier that year the US space program was preparing its astronauts for flight to the moon when tragedy struck. In January, during a practice countdown, astronauts Virgil Grissom, Edward White and Roger Chaffee were killed when a flash fire swept through the command module. The program was delayed while safety modifications were made. The Apollo 7 mission was finally launched in October of 1968, and the spacecraft was checked out while in earth orbit. After three more orbiting test flights, the Apollo 11 spacecraft was launched on July 16, 1969, and successfully reached the moon. Astronauts Neil Armstrong and Ed Aldrin, assisted by Michael Collins, became the first men to step onto the surface of the moon, returning safely to earth a week later.

A proud country rallied around the returning heroes to celebrate one of the greatest achievements in the history of mankind. And through it all and beyond, *Apollo* pinball machines had stood out in the arcades, pool halls and bowling alleys across the country.

This pinball game enjoyed an exceptionally long popularity, not only because it followed on the vapor trail of the space program, but because it played exceptionally well. Renowned for its long shots and side channels, *Apollo* was usually played to death in most locations where hardcore pin addicts hung out. Most examples still on location by early 1969 showed extended signs of wear from excessive play, so clean copies of this game are scarce and should be considered premium.

■ *A BACKGLASS PANORAMA OF POWER*

Hovering in a helicopter a quarter mile from a rocket launching must be a vibrant, majestic experience! That's exactly the effect conveyed by *Apollo's* backglass, with considerable success. As if watching from the air, set back behind the control tower, we can survey the entire scene.

Inside the tower, while the diligent personnel carry out their duties during liftoff, a military official gazes in awe as the Apollo spacecraft emerges from its underground launch chamber in a surge of billowing smoke and flame. Off in the distance spreads the deep blue ocean, curving away to the cloud-covered horizon. Observation craft hang nearby in the air and float upon the sea as they monitor the progress of the launch. An auxiliary launching pad stands a mile away, perhaps in readiness for the next mission.

Central in the left side of the backglass is the animation display, an inset area similar to a vertical bagatelle. It consists of a launching alley emanating from the nose of the rocket in the picture, leading into a field of separated pins, which channel down into five roll-through slots. The outer two are labeled for 50 points, the inner pair are worth 300 points, and the center slot is labeled for S P E C I A L, a free game.

Quite an amazing perspective to fit into a picture less than two feet square! Nonetheless, the effect is stunning, especially when the scene is illuminated by turning on the game in a dark room. This is further enhanced by installing flasher lights behind the name APOLLO so that the fiery red letters twinkle and glow.

■ *WORKING UP TO A COUNTDOWN* Game play priorities on *Apollo* are simple but captivating. The main focus is upon making "advances" by hitting several different targets. There are four yellow 10-point advance buttons, and a single yellow advance button at top center worth 100 points. The round "dead" bumper at the very top of the playfield is also an advance when lit. And last, the string of rollover buttons which climb the middle of the playfield will have one at a time lit to indicate where the

OPPOSITE Space Shuttle *was from Zaccaria, not to be confused with the game of the same name from Williams.*

"Your senses will never be the same!"

WIZARD

BY *Bally* OF COURSE

-PLAYER FLIPPER

CONVERTIBLE TO ADD-A-BALL

ANN-MARGRET, the star of TOMMY, a Columbia motion picture, enjoys the company of WIZARD, which was inspired by TOMMY.

"countdown" sits; this one is also worth an advance.

When the countdown advances to "1" the top center yellow button lights for 300 points. One more advance will bring the countdown back to "10" and light the LAUNCH ROCKET indicator by the flippers. Hitting the top yellow button awards the points and increases the point values for the central rocket button targets and the side outlanes. Continuing to make advances will bring the countdown up to "1" again and enable you to again increase the playfield scoring values. Yet a third time will maximize point profit so that the two rocket targets alter nate for 100 and 300 points, and the outlanes alternate for 300 points and SPECIAL.

An additional benefit of nailing the lighted countdown target is the opening of the gate on the right side outlane. This nifty little device diverts the ball back to the plunger alley instead of draining, thus allowing you a reprieve from the usual end of ball in play. Although the gate is supposed to close, triggered by the returned ball's weight upon a switch in the alley, devious players like myself have discovered that with perfect plunger timing, the ball can be reshot without its weight depressing the switch, thus keeping the gate open for the next round. Cheating? Hardly! My philosophy contends that you deserve whatever you can milk from the game, short of physical damage. Man versus machine, right?

■ *BLAST OFF FOR EXTRA REWARDS* Upon losing the ball to the outhole, if you have advanced past the "1" to the "10," watch the backglass animation display for a rocket launch! POINK! A tiny steel ball flies up into the space above the pins and jitterbugs its way down toward the slots. With a little Body English you may persuade it to keep toward the center of the field and hit a 300-point slot or maybe even the SPECIAL. This reward can make a

OPPOSITE Wizard *was designed by* Greg Kmiec *and with art from* Dave Christensen, *another Bally beauty.*

considerable difference in your game, especially if you rack up a couple of replays just for watching the steel ball whiz into action.

Apollo has two amazing shots which can really rack up the points in short order. First is the great long shot from the flippers straight up the middle of the playfield to smack the center advance button. This shot is reinforced by the row of rollover buttons, which act as a conduction path to keep the ball on a straight and true path toward its destination, and coupled with the highly responsive flippers, one can actually cause an airborne silverball upon impact!

The second shot is a bi-directional situation which makes use of what was an innovation back in 1967. The left and right side channels with the funky rockets at their entrances make for some extremely high point scoring if you get your rhythm and speed just right. Either flipper can send the ball swooping up an opposite side channel to collect 100 or 300 points, and if the altitude is correct upon its emergence at the top of the playfield, the ball will cross over to the top entrance for the channel on the other side. Thus you get a return to the flippers and 200 or 400 points. If your reflexes are in good shape, you can send the ball back for another orbit and more points to help you on your way to more replays.

Since *Apollo* typically requires about 3,500 points for the first replay, and up to three more may be awarded by the time you reach 6,000 points, these side alleys will get you there by leaps and bounds! A special situation, in which the ball only gets enough juice to slide up and sit on top of the rollover switch, can cause the scoring motor in the machine to dish out up to 800 points.

Although most favorite and preferred pinballs of the sixties were designed by Gottlieb, Williams was responsible for a few gems. *Apollo* is definitely one of them. Combined with its historical theme and animation, this machine's exceptional playability ranks it right up on top. Watch for it, or its add-a-ball cousin, *Blastoff.*

Another excellent example of Christensen's work, this time reflecting the artist's circle of friends, is *Nitro Groundshaker* (Bally 1979). Not only does this game have associates of a motorcycle club depicted in the spectator stand of the drag-racing scenes, with some dubious goings on – especially in the grandstand bearing the legend "Dragster City," but also acknowledges colleagues at Bally, among them Norm Clark.

Credited, in jest, in the design as "Mechanic," Norm Clark, much revered in the world of pinball, was the Head of Pinball Design at Bally. Other Bally personalities that have been acknowledged in Christensen's art include Ed Schmidt, Service Engineer extraordinaire, and W. T. O'Donnell.

The artist's sense of humor has not always been restricted to the tameness of people parachuting from an airplane, in the background to *Bon Voyage*. On more than one occasion it has been the cause of concern to Bally. Sometimes the innuendo of *Nitro Groundshaker* has upset the sensibilities of influential people. Such a case was *Captain Fantastic*, where a last minute modification, in the shape of stars over the offending parts, had to be made. Although many thousand examples of this game were distributed, legend has it that only sixty of the unmodified glasses still exist.

Of the machines mentioned so far, *Wizard*, *Bon Voyage* and *Nitro Groundshaker* all provide excellent examples of Dave's obsession with buckles; this is only one area of detail among many, in which this artist continues the pinball tradition.

Next time you are close to a pinball machine give the backglass a second look – you might be surprised by some of the unusual things you can find buried in the detail!

THE ART OF DAVE CHRISTENSEN

Fireball is recognized by connoisseurs to be the zenith of electromechanical pinball machine design. Much of its reputation is due to its particularly stunning artwork designed by the maestro of 1970's pinball artwork – Dave "Mad Dog" Christensen.

This machine displayed Dave Christensen's first pinball art to go into production, but was not typical of the style which he later developed and is uniquely recognizable as his own. He describes his style as the three B's – broads, boobs and buckles. Check out the backglasses of games such as *Bon Voyage* (Bally 1974), *Wizard* (Bally 1975), and you will see why.

Christensen's art is an extension of comic book stuff and as such provides precisely the right sort of embellishment to accompany the pinball game. His art is fun, perverse, brash, dynamic and amusing. The very same adjectives that could be used to describe the best pinball games.

Typical of the artist's perverseness is the way Adolf Hitler makes a cameo appearance in the crowd scene that decorates the backglass of *Captain Fantastic* (Bally 1976). This game featured the rock star Elton John as the main character and while it obviously capitalized on Elton John's contemporary success, the inclusion of Adolf Hitler acknowledges, but does not glorify, the topical interest in Nazism.

ABOVE LEFT *Dave Christensen (right) and Greg Kmiec, with the machine they created 10 years before.*

OPPOSITE *Bally's Twin Win – official and original version (inset, above), Spot Adolf Hitler, included for no particular reason in the back glass of Capt. Fantastic.*

THE TOKEN GESTURE IN PINBALL

Rewards granted by pinball machines have taken on many guises during pinball's half century of public enjoyment. Unfortunately this has led to bad stigmas and a spotted past in many regions of the United States. The first few years of coin-operated production in the 1930s saw numerous manufacturers of slot machines jumping onto the pinwagon. This resulted in a wide variety of games which dispensed coins as rewards for skillful play (of course, a little luck helps also). Many other new manufacturers of pinballs followed suit to stay in the competition.

The original coin-payout pinballs gave out legal tender for their returns, starting in about 1933. Within two years there was a wide variety of payout machines. But the law was forcing manufacturers to jump back and forth across the dividing line between amusement games and payout games. The alternative to eliminating coin payouts was to dispense different rewards, so the player was given a return which was not "spendable." Here's a bit about one method which was very prevalent, if only for a short time.

I went back to Arkansas in the summer of 1987 to visit friends in the north part of the state – the "playground of the Ozarks." One of my visits was to see Wayne Neyens, the former Gottlieb playfield designer, creator of many classic games of the fifties and sixties. I had asked him if he had any interesting mementos of his early days to show me, and he had managed to dig out some early photos from his days both as a designer and as head of the Gottlieb engineering department. There were miscellaneous shots of some of the other engineers, of Alvin Gottlieb, and of the unique *Challenger* two-ended machine developed in 1971.

But the most fascinating item he showed me was a small round, flat container, like a talcum-powder box, full to the brim of metal tokens. There were several

hundred at least. They varied in size from a penny to a nickel, some being brass or bronze, some copper. Others were minted from some silvery metal, though not silver. Quite a few had holes or some other cutout through the middle. There were many with a "5" stamped in the center of one side. A lot of them bore variations on the slogan "No Cash Value" or "Good For Free Play Only." I began to recognize the names of some of the amusement-machine manufacturers on several, but many more had the names of commercial establishments on them. A surprising proportion of the coins were still as shiny and fresh-looking as a brand new penny.

After sifting through a couple of handfuls, I picked out a representative sample for photographic purposes. Wayne proceeded to fill me in on what he remembered about them. Before he went to work for Gottlieb in 1939, he had been employed at Western Equipment and Supply, another manufacturer of coin-operated machines in Chicago. From 1936–39 Wayne was an all-round handyman at this company, though he had originally been hired as a draftsman. One of his numerous duties was to "recondition" games returned from location to the company. "We didn't exactly rebuilt the games," recalled Wayne, "we just replaced the dry cell batteries which had invariably gone bad, and checked for correct operation. There wasn't too much that could go wrong with them, as simple as they were back then. But often there were still nickels left inside, so whoever reworked the machine might find a handful. I usually made an effort to volunteer for fixing up the returned pingames in hopes of getting lucky. And there were almost always some of those darn tokens inside the game, which didn't do us any good at all. Most often they got thrown out, but sometimes I would toss them into a container. That's how I saved up these ones I have here."

Tokens, or "checks" as they were also known, were an interim effort between coin payouts and ticket-vendor payouts, to give the pinball player a

tangible reward with some kind of value. They were only prevalent in payout pins for a year or two (approximately 1937–38) and then were outlawed, just as other methods of payouts would eventually fall before the law.

Each establishment would have its own legend or identifying mark on its checks, which were dispensed by the pingame for skillful achievement. Others were supplied by the coin machine manufacturer, with their legend stamped on them. The coin entry to the game would accept either real coins or the checks, which were then separated by a discriminating mechanism inside. The coins were channeled into the cashbox, and the checks were diverted into the payout tube for dispensing again to the player. Thus all real money was retained without recycle,

LEFT *Tokens from various manufacturers, a compromise between cash payout and "for amusement only."*

ABOVE *Assembly of pintables is a more complex and streamlined business than it was in Wayne Neyens' time.*

and the token reward could be spent only at the establishment, in trade or for free play.

Or so they would have you think! It soon became apparent that the checks were considered the equivalent of money at some places and could be exchanged for cash by sneaky cashiers. Sometimes the coin-token separator mechanism would fail to discriminate correctly and channel nickels off into the check payout tube. Accident? Maybe sometimes, but probably not all the time! Once it became obvious to the legal watchdogs that tokens were only a substitute for money in many places, the crackdown began. The law soon detected the real intention behind the checks and deemed their use illegal. They went as quickly as they had come, leaving many businesses with a small-scale coin minting operation in progress that would never be worth anything to them again.

At this point the pinball companies had to find a way to give skill rewards that didn't simulate a coin. They next turned to ticket and mint vendors, but these also attracted the attention of law enforcers. It was only with the invention and continued implementation of the free play and add-a-ball mechanisms that pinball eventually freed itself from the bad vibes which threatened to make it illegal to play. Whew! That was pretty close – what if we only had fond memories of the way our folks used to play these pingames back in the thirties and forties? Let us all be glad there were persistent pinball companies and inventors those days.

THE WORLD OF PINBALL MAKERS

Williams, Bally, Gottlieb and Data East all manufacture pinball machines in Chicago. Between them they must produce 90%-plus of the world's output. Chicago has a long history as the world's major producer of pinball games. However, it is not the sole geographic location of this industry. Atari, the first of the major hi-tech pinball makers, had their manufacturing facility on the West Coast; over fifty years ago there was a flourishing pinball industry in Ohio.

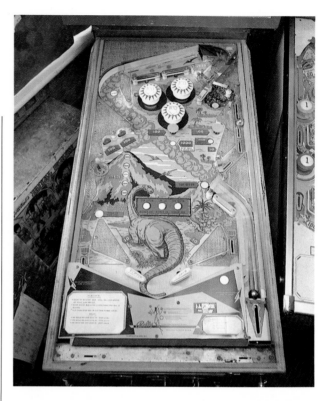

ABOVE *This example of* Four Million B.C. *was for export to Germany, a market large enough to justify translation. The ball does not enter in the conventional way,* *as you can see, but across the playfield from right to left.*
RIGHT West Club *from Rally is one of the few examples of machines not made in Chicago.*

But what about the rest of the world? Surprisingly, Japan often perceived to be at the forefront in the world of technological wizardry, has not been able to maintain a pinball industry. That is not to say there is no demand for pinball in Japan. The Japanese pinball market is serviced by imports from Chicago.

Europe has been more successful, particularly in recent years. Looking for early stirrings, the earliest games resembling the machines of this century must be those assembled by the Exhibit Supply Company at the Hong Kong Works, Wembley, England, in the early thirties.

We then jump forward to the 1950s, when Williams and Bally were exporting parts to Ireland where they were assembled into complete machines for re-export to England, and probably other parts of Europe. The reason for this practice was to exploit the differential in taxes on complete machines, which was higher than the tax on component parts.

In the sixties, a French company called Rally was arguably leading the world of pinball design. Rally

and "Rockmakers," which was based on the Flintstones. Unfortunately they were ahead of their time and the rest of the world wasn't ready to follow. Rally were extremely innovative; they challenged all the previously held concepts of pinball design and technology.

The obvious differences between their games and those from Chicago were digital scoring, which was achieved by the use of Decade counters, electronically synthesized sound, and crystal colored playfield parts. Their bumper design was stunning both cosmetically and technically. Here again they used translucent colored plastic (which started to appear on American games over fifteen years later). They did not use the conventional bumper shape. For the first time rectangular bumpers were introduced, three was born out of a company that made radar and electronic components. They started with three electromechanical games which included "Beatniks"

inches long and half an inch wide. The Rally bumpers were the first to use DC current, this meant not only that they were more responsive, but they had more energy with which to propel the ball. Once again, some years later, DC current started to be utilized by the manufacturers in Chicago in the operation of the bumpers on their pingames.

Rally's new generation of pingames included such titles as *West Club*, *Playboy* – a two player game, *Schusse* and *Flower Child* – a four-player game which utilized electromagnets to propel the ball back up the playfield. There was also a game called *Comics* which was produced in prototype form, as a six-player game, but this was never commercially produced.

In the 1970s the pinball world went crazy, well perhaps not the whole world but specifically Italy and Spain. In these countries new companies started producing pinball machines primarily for their home markets; some of these games made their way to other

Two games from the successful Italian company, Zaccaria (now Technoplay); their machines are popular mainly in the UK, but their percentage of world markets is tiny.

European countries and some, like those from Zaccaria from Italy, were successful in the USA. Once again, an important incentive to produce machines "locally" must have been the avoidance of import taxes; in addition there was of course the motivation of saving the costs of transatlantic transportation.

Manufacture in Italy and Spain still continues today. Primarily, the machines are used within the country of origin, with the exception of Technoplay (previously Zaccaria) games, popular in the UK.

Historically, games of European origin were a very mixed bunch; some were original designs of variable quality, while others were copies of games designed in the USA and made under licence. An example of the latter is *High Speed*, originally designed by Steve Ritchie and manufactured by Williams, in Chicago, also produced under license by Unidesa of Spain. It is interesting to note that the Spanish versions of USA games are not always identical to the original.

For example, Williams' *Flash*, a four-player electronic game when made in the USA, was produced in Spain as a single player game called *Storm*. Perhaps surprisingly, while the USA manufacturers have gone out of their way to produce foreign language versions of their games for the European market, especially the talking games, the Spanish and Italian makers tend to manufacture English language games.

In the 1980s, in addition to the Spanish and Italian manufacturers there has also been production in France and Germany. In France, a company previously known for its video games, Jeutel, branched out into the production of pintables of its own designs. In Germany, for a short time, Bally collaborated with Wulff to manufacture original Bally-USA designs. Some of the games produced include *Cybernaut, Eight Ball Champ* and *Fireball Classic*.

Another development in the 1980s were games with different artwork but the same game play as USA games. These games are made under licence in Europe. The leading manufacturer in this field is Bell Games, Spain, who produced *Fantasy*, which was originally released by Bally as *Centaur, World Defender*, previously released by Williams as *Laser Cue* and *Space Hawks*, a remake of Bally's *Cybernaut*. These games were designed as update kits. That is, the game would be purchased in kit form to be installed in an older game; because this would utilize many original parts as well as the cabinet, in effect it gave the user a new game at a much reduced price.

One variation on this theme came from a German company called Arkon. They produced a conversion kit based on Bally's *Playboy*. The kit, which offered the game called *"Sexy Girl,"* had the innovative feature of a projection system under the playfield. This provided a full-color pin-up show, based on a library of two hundred pictures, which changed each time a target was hit by the silver ball. Conversion games have had limited impact on the market because in general they lack the feel, original sound effects and artistic appeal of the games they are based upon.

Manufacturers that have produced games in Europe in the last twenty years:

Manufacturer	Games	Country
INDER	Hot and Cold	Spain
INTERFLIP	Alaska	Germany
JOCTRONIC	Punky Willy	Spain
JUEGOS POPULARES	Aqualand	Spain
	Halley Comet	
KOMPLETT FLIPPER	Space Rider	Germany
	Fly High	
MAGUINAS	Mac's Galaxy	Spain
	Mac Jungle	
	Space Train	
MARTEL	Terry's	Spain
NORDOMATIC	Monte Carlo	Spain
NSM	Cosmic Flash	Germany
	Firebirds	
PETACO	Comodin	Spain
PEYPER	Wolf Man	Spain
PLAYMATIC	Geisha	Spain
RECEL	Fortune	Spain
	Lady Luck	
	Master Stroke	
	Top Racer	
	Torpedo	
ROYAL	Escape	Holland
RUMATIC	Mini Flipper	Spain
	(The playfield is a video screen)	
SEGASA	Monaco	Spain
SONIC	Pole Position	Spain
	Butterfly	
	Mars Trek	
	Prospector	
	Super Straight	
STARGAME	White Force	Spain
TECHNOPLAY	Scramble	Italy
	X Force	
UNIDESA	High Speed	Spain
ZACCARIA	Aerobatics	Italy
	Blackbelt	
	Clown	
	Combat	
	Devil Riders	
	Magic Castle	
	Moon Flight	
	Pool Champion	
	Robot	
	Pinball Champ	
	Soccer Kings	
	Supersonic	
	Ten Stars	
	Universe	
	Wood's Queen	

50 YEARS OF PINBALL

This is a comprehensive list of all pinball machines manufactured in the US from 1939 onward. The dominance of the "Big Three" – Bally, Gottlieb and Williams – is immediately apparent. The number of players is indicated (*2P* = 2 players) together with year of distribution and the month, where known.

ASTRO GAMES

79 BLACK SHEEP SQUADRON *4P*

BALLY

8/39 CHAMPION
1/46 SURF QUEENS
4/47 ROCKET
7/47 SILVER STREAK
48 CARNIVAL
48 EUREKA
48 BALLERINA
48 RANCHO
1/48 MELODY
1/48 MELODY ROLL
8/56 BALLS-A-POPPIN *2P*
2/63 MOON SHOT
3/63 CROSS COUNTRY
7/63 CUE TEASE *2P*
7/63 3-IN-LINE *4P*
11/63 HOOTENANNY
12/63 STAR JET *2P*
2/64 MONTE CARLO
3/64 BONGO *2P*
4/64 SKY DIVERS
5/64 MAD WORLD *2P*
6/64 GRAND TOUR
6/64 HAPPY TOUR
7/64 2 IN 1 *2P*
8/64 BIG DAY *4P*
10/64 HARVEST
10/64 HAYRIDE
12/64 BUS STOP *2P*
65 BULLS EYE
1/65 BULL FIGHT
2/65 SHEBA *2P*
3/65 BAND WAGON *4P*
6/65 MAGIC CIRCLE
7/65 50/50 *2P*
8/65 ACES HIGH *4P*
9/65 DISCOTECK *2P*
11/65 TRIO
12/65 BLUE RIBBON *4P*
66 SIX SHOOTER
2/66 WILD WHEELS *2P*
3/66 SIX STICKS *6P*
4/66 GOLD RUSH
8/66 CAMPUS QUEEN *4P*
10/66 BAZAAR
10/66 LOOP-THE-LOOP *2P*
12/66 CAPERSVILLE *4P*
67 HEAT WAVE
67 BOOT-A-BALL
4/67 ROCKET III
8/67 THE WIGGLER *4P*
12/67 SURFERS
1/68 DOGGIES *4P*
4/68 DIXIELAND
5/68 SAFARI *2P*
8/68 ROCK MAKERS *4P*

11/68 MINI-ZAG
12/68 ALLIGATOR
69 TEN PIN
1/69 COSMOS *4P*
4/69 OP-POP-POP
6/69 GATOR *4P*
8/69 ON BEAM
9/69 JOUST *2P*
11/69 BALLY HOO *4P*
12/69 KING TUT
1/70 KING REX
2/70 CAMELOT *4P*
2/70 GALAHAD *2P*
4/70 BOWL-O
5/70 BIG VALLEY *4P*
8/70 ZIP-A-DOO *2P*
9/70 TRAIL DRIVE
11/70 SEE-SAW *4P*
12/70 4 QUEENS
1/71 VAMPIRE *2P*
2/71 FIRECRACKER *4P*
5/71 FOUR MILLION B C *4P*
5/71 SKY ROCKET *2P*
8/71 EXPRESSWAY
10/71 SEA RAY *2P*
11/71 MARINER *4P*
72 RED MAX
2/72 FIREBALL *4P*
4/72 EL TORO
8/72 LITTLE JOE *4P*
10/72 SPACE TIME *4P*
10/72 TIME TUNNEL *4P*
73 ROUND UP *2P*
73 FORE
73 BALI-HI *4P*
3/73 MONTE CARLO *4P*
3/73 ODDS & EVENS
5/73 TIME ZONE *2P*
7/73 NIP-IT *4P*
10/73 HI-LO ACE
11/73 CIRCUS *4P*
1/74 BIG SHOW *2P*
2/74 CHAMP *4P*
2/74 TWIN WIN *2P*
4/74 SKY KINGS
5/74 AMIGO *4P*
7/74 DELTA QUEEN
8/74 ROGO *4P*
11/74 BON VOYAGE
12/74 BOOMERANG *4P*
1/75 FLICKER *2P*
2/75 AIR ACES *4P*
4/75 KNOCKOUT *2P*
5/75 WIZARD *4P*
10/75 HI DEAL
11/75 BOW AND ARROW *4P*
76 SLAPSTICK
1/76 FLIP FLOP *4P*
3/76 HOKUS POKUS *2P*
4/76 OLD CHICAGO *4P*
6/76 ALADDIN'S CASTLE *2P*
6/76 CAPTAIN FANTASTIC *4P*
6/76 FREEDOM *4P*
6/76 KICK-OFF *4P*
9/76 QUARTERBACK *2P*
12/76 HANG GLIDER *4P*
3/77 NIGHT RIDER *4P*
6/77 EVIL KNIEVEL *4P*
9/77 EIGHT BALL *4P*
1/78 POWER PLAY *4P*
4/78 MATA HARI *4P*

6/78 BLACK JACK *4P*
6/78 STRIKES AND SPARES *4P*
8/78 LOST WORLD *4P*
10/78 SIX MILLION DOLLAR MAN *6P*
12/78 PLAYBOY *4P*
2/79 VOLTAN *4P*
3/79 SUPERSONIC *4P*
4/79 STAR TREK *4P*
6/79 KISS *4P*
6/79 PARAGON *4P*
9/79 HARLEM GLOBETROTTERS *4P*
11/79 DOLLY PARTON *4P*
12/79 FUTURE SPA *4P*
1/80 NITRO GROUNDSHAKER *4P*
2/80 SILVERBALL MANIA *4P*
3/80 SPACE INVADERS *4P*
5/80 ROLLING STONES *4P*
6/80 HOT DOGGIN *4P*
6/80 MYSTIC *4P*
7/80 VIKING *4P*
11/80 SKATEBALL *4P*
12/80 FRONTIER *4P*
12/80 XENON *4P*
1/81 FLASH GORDON *4P*
3/81 8 BALL DELUXE *4P*
5/81 FIREBALL II *4P*
6/81 EMBRYON *4P*
9/81 FATHOM *4P*
10/81 MEDUSA *4P*
11/81 CENTAUR *4P*
12/81 ELEKTRA *4P*
82 BMX *4P*
2/82 VECTOR *4P*
5/82 MR & MRS PAC-MAN *4P*
8/82 SPEAK EASY *2P*
8/82 SPECTRUM *4P*
10/82 BABY PAC MAN
10/82 EIGHT BALL DELUXE LE *4P*
83 GRAND SLAM *4P*
6/83 CENTAUR II *4P*
10/83 GOLD BALL *4P*
1/84 GRANNY AND THE GATORS *2P*
3/84 X'S AND O'S *4P*
5/84 KINGS OF STEEL *4P*
7/84 BLACK PYRAMID *4P*
10/84 SPY HUNTER *4P*
2/85 FIREBALL CLASSIC *4P*
5/85 CYBERNAUT *4P*
9/85 EIGHT BALL CHAMP *4P*
11/85 BEAT THE CLOCK *4P*
2/86 LADY LUCK *4P*
4/86 MOTORDOME *4P*
6/86 BLACK BELT *4P*
6/86 KARATE FIGHT *4P*
8/86 SPECIAL FORCE *4P*
10/86 STRANGE SCIENCE *4P*
3/87 CITY SLICKER *4P*
4/87 HARDBODY *4P*
6/87 PARTY ANIMAL *4P*
8/87 HEAVY METAL MELTDOWN *4P*
10/87 DUNGEONS AND DRAGONS *4P*
1/88 ESCAPE FROM THE LOST WORLD *4P*
3/88 BLACKWATER 100 *4P*

CENTURY GAMES

78 STAR BATTLE *2P*

DATA EAST

8/87 LAZER WAR *4P*
3/88 SECRET SERVICE *4P*

EXHIBIT

48 MIMI
48 BANJO
48 JAMBOREE
48 SAMBA
48 SHORT STOP
48 CIRCUS
48 CONTACT
48 MOROCCO
48 MAGIC
1/48 BUILD UP
49 SWANEE
49 GONDOLA
49 PLAYTIME
49 TUMBLEWEED
49 SHANTYTOWN
50 CAMPUS
50 BE BOP
50 JEANIE
50 JUDY
50 PLAYLAND
50 OASIS

FASCINATION GAME

79 THE ENTERTAINER *2P*
79 EROS II *2P*

GAME PLAN

78 FAMILY FUN *4P*
78 FOXY LADY *4P*
78 SHARPSHOOTER *4P*
78 BLACK VELVET *4P*
78 STAR TRIP *4P*
78 REAL *4P*
79 CONEY ISLAND *4P*
79 VEGAS *4P*
81 LIZZARD *4P*
6/81 GLOBAL WARFARE *4P*
82 MIKE BOSSY *4P*
82 SUPER NOVA *4P*
10/84 SHARPSHOOTER II *4P*
12/84 ATTILA THE HUN *4P*
3/85 AGENTS 777 *4P*
3/85 LADY SHARPSHOOTER *4P*
4/85 CAPTAIN HOOK *4P*
9/85 ANDROMEDA *4P*
11/85 CYCLOPES *4P*
11/85 LOCH NESS MONSTER *4P*

GENCO

10/47 BRONCHO
48 TRADE WINDS
48 MARDI GRAS
48 MERRY WIDOW
48 MERRY WIDOW
48 SCREW BALL
48 ONE, TWO, THREE
48 PUDDIN' HEAD
48 BONE HEAD
48 FLOATING POWER
1/48 TRIPLE ACTION
49 BIG TOP
49 BLACK GOLD
49 THREE FEATHERS
49 CAMEL CARAVAN
49 RIP SNORTER
50 SOUTH PACIFIC

50 MERCURY
50 ROCKET
50 CANASTA
50 HARVEST TIME
50 FLYING SAUCERS
51 TRI-SCORE
51 SPORTSMAN
51 HIT AND RUN
51 STOP AND GO
52 DOUBLE ACTION
52 SPRINGTIME
52 400
52 JUMPING JACK
53 GOLDEN NUGGET
53 SILVER CHEST
54 INVADERS
57 FUN FAIR

GRAND PRODUCTS

86 BULLSEYE 301 *4P*

KEENEY

12/47 COVER GIRL
49 BAND LEADER
51 HOLIDAY
52 LITE-A-LINE
53 DOMINO BOWLER
63 GO CART
8/63 POKER FACE
9/63 ARROWHEAD *2P*
11/63 COLORAMA *2P*

KOMPUTER DYNAMICS

10/71 INVASION STRATEGY *2P*

MIDWAY

63 FLYING TURNS *2P*
9/63 RACE WAY *2P*
64 RODEO *2P*
78 ROTATION VIII *4P*

MIRCO

75 SPIRIT OF 76 *2P*

PINSTAR

85 GAMATRON *4P*

PREMIER TECHNOLOGY

(Gottlieb changed its name to Premier Technology in 1984)

10/47 HUMPTY DUMPTY
1/48 LADY ROBIN HOOD
3/48 CINDERELLA
4/48 JACK AND JILL
5/48 KING COLE
6/48 ALI BABA
8/48 ALICE IN WONDERLAND
8/48 BARNACLE BILL
10/48 BUCCANEER
11/48 ROUND UP
12/48 ONE TWO THREEE
12/48 HARVEST MOON
1/49 TELECARD
2/49 GIN RUMMY
2/49 BOWLING CHAMP
2/49 OLD FAITHFUL
3/49 BUTTONS AND BOWS
5/49 SHARPSHOOTER
6/49 DOUBLE SHUFFLE
7/49 THREE MUSKETEERS
8/49 COLLEGE DAYS
10/49 KING ARTHUR
10/49 BASKETBALL
11/49 K. C. JONES
1/50 JUST 21
4/50 SELECT-A-CARD

5/50 BANK-A-BALL
5/50 BUFFALO BILL
6/50 MADISON SQUARE GARDEN
7/50 TRIPLETS
8/50 ROCKETTES
9/50 FOUR HORSEMEN
10/50 SPOT BOWLER
11/50 JOKER
12/50 DOUBLE FEATURE
12/50 KNOCK OUT
2/51 MINSTREL MAN
3/51 HAPPY-GO-LUCKY
4/51 CYCLONE
5/51 MERMAID
7/51 GLAMOR
8/51 WILD WEST
10/51 ROSE-BOWL
11/51 GLOBE TROTTER
12/51 NIAGARA
1/52 ALL-STAR BASKETBALL
2/52 QUARTETTE
3/52 HIT N RUN
5/52 CROSS ROADS
6/52 FOUR STARS
7/52 HAPPY DAYS
8/52 SKILL-POOL
10/52 CHINATOWN
11/52 CORONATION
12/52 QUEEN OF HEARTS
2/53 FLYING HIGH
3/53 QUINTETTE
4/53 GRAND SLAM
5/53 GUYS AND DOLLS
6/53 MARBLE QUEEN
8/53 POKER FACE
9/53 SHINDIG
10/53 PIN WHEEL
11/53 ARABIAN KNIGHTS
54 RICCOCHET
1/54 GREEN PASTURES
2/54 LOVELY LUCY
3/54 MYSTIC MARVEL
4/54 JOCKEY CLUB
5/54 HAWAIIAN BEAUTY
6/54 DRAGONETTE
7/54 DAISY MAY
8/54 GOLD STAR
9/54 LADY LUCK
10/54 SUPER JUMBO *4P*
10/54 4-BELLES
10/54 DELUXE JUMBO *4P*
11/54 STAGE COACH
12/54 DIAMOND LILL
55 DELUXE SLUGGIN CHAMP
1/55 TWIN-BILL
2/55 GYPSY QUEEN
3/55 DUETTE *2P*
4/55 SLUGGIN CHAMP
5/55 JUBILEE *4P*
6/55 SOUTHERN BELLE
7/55 SWEET-ADD-A-LINE
8/55 TOURNAMENT *2P*
9/55 WISHING WELL
10/55 MARATHON *2P*
11/55 FRONTIERSMAN
12/55 EASY ACES
1/56 GLADIATOR *2P*
2/56 HARBOR LITES
3/56 SCORE-BOARD *4P*
4/56 DERBY DAY
6/56 TOREADOR *2P*
7/56 CLASSY BOWLER
8/56 SEA BELLES *2P*
9/56 AUTO RACE
10/56 REGISTER *4P*
11/56 FAIR LADY *2P*
12/56 RAINBOW
1/57 FLAG-SHIP *2P*
2/57 ACE HIGH
3/57 MAJESTIC *4P*
4/57 ROYAL FLUSH

6/57 CONTINENTAL CAFE *2P*
8/57 WORLD CHAMP
10/57 SUPER CIRCUS *2P*
11/57 FALSTAFF *4P*
11/57 SILVER
12/57 STRAIGHT FLUSH
1/58 WHIRL WIND *2P*
2/58 CRISS CROSS
3/58 BRITE STAR *2P*
4/58 ROCKET SHIP
6/58 PICNIC *2P*
7/58 ROTO POOL
8/58 GONDOLIER *2P*
9/58 SUNSHINE
10/58 CONTEST *4P*
11/58 SITTIN PRETTY
12/58 DOUBLE ACTION *2P*
1/59 STRAIGHT SHOOTER
3/59 RACE TIME *2P*
4/59 HIGH DIVER
5/59 ATLAS *2P*
6/59 QUEEN OF DIAMONDS
7/59 AROUND THE WORLD *2P*
8/59 MISS ANNABELLE
9/59 SWEET SIOUX *4P*
10/59 UNIVERSE
11/59 MADEMOISELLE *2P*
12/59 LIGHTING BALL
12/59 SEVEN SEAS *2P*
1/60 WORLD BEAUTIES
2/60 LITE-A-CARD *2P*
3/60 WAGON TRAIN
4/60 TEXAN *4P*
5/60 DANCING DOLLS
6/60 CAPTAIN KIDD *2P*
8/60 SPOT-A-CARDI
9/60 MELODY LANE *2P*
10/60 KEWPIE DOLL
11/60 FLIPPER
12/60 MERRY-GO-ROUND *2P*
1/61 FOTO-FINISH
2/61 OKLAHOMA *4P*
4/61 SHOW BOAT
5/61 FLIPPER PARADE
6/61 FLYING CIRCUS *2P*
8/61 BIG CASINO
9/61 LANCER *2P*
10/61 CORRAL
11/61 FLIPPER FAIR
12/61 ALOHA *2P*
1/62 EGG HEAD
1/62 FLIPPER COWBOY
2/62 LIBERTY BELLE *4P*
4/62 FLIPPER CLOWN
5/62 TROPIC ISLE
6/62 FASHION SHOW *2P*
7/62 COVER GIRL
8/62 PREVIEW *2P*
9/62 OLYMPICS *2P*
11/62 SUNSET *2P*
12/62 RACK-A-BALL
1/63 GAUCHO *4P*
4/63 SLICK CHICK
6/63 SQUARE HEAD
7/63 SWING ALONG *2P*
9/63 SWEET HEARTS
10/63 FLYING CHARIOTS *2P*
1/64 BIG TOP *2P*
1/64 GIGI
2/64 SHIP-MATES *4P*
4/64 WORLD FAIR
6/64 BONANZA *2P*
7/64 BOWLING GREEN
8/64 MAJORETTES
8/64 SEA SHORE *2P*
9/64 NORTH STAR
11/64 HAPPY CLOWN *4P*
1/65 SKY LINE
2/65 THORO-BRED *2P*
3/65 KINGS & QUEENS
4/65 HI DOLLY *2P*

5/65 COWPOKE
6/65 BUCKAROO
6/65 RANCHO
7/65 DODGE CITY *4P*
9/65 BANK-A-BALLI
10/65 FLIPPER POOL
10/65 ELEKTRA POOL
11/65 PARADISE *2P*
12/65 ICE REVUE
12/65 PLEASURE ISLE
66 HYDE PARK
1/66 HAWAIIAN ISLE
1/66 ICE SHOW
1/66 MASQUERADE *4P*
4/66 CENTRAL PARK
5/66 HURDY GURDY
6/66 MAYFAIR *2P*
10/66 CROSS TOWN
10/66 SUBWAY
12/66 DANCING LADY *4P*
2/67 KING OF DIAMONDS
2/67 SOLITAIRE
2/67 HIT-A-CARD
4/67 DIAMOND JACK
5/67 SUPER SCORE *2P*
7/67 HI-SCORE *4P*
7/67 SUPER DUO
8/67 HARMONY
10/67 MELODY
10/67 SING ALONG
11/67 TROUBADOUR
12/67 SURF SIDE *2P*
12/67 SEA SIDE *2P*
2/68 ROYAL GUARD
3/68 PALACE GUARD
3/68 ELITE GUARD
5/68 FUN LAND
5/68 SPIN WHEEL *4P*
8/68 FUN FAIR
8/68 FUN PARK
8/68 TIVOLI
9/68 PAUL BUNYAN *2P*
10/68 BIG JACK
10/68 DOMINO
10/68 GRANDE DOMINO
12/68 PLAYMATES
69 SUPER BOWL
1/69 FOUR SEASONS *4P*
2/69 SPIN-A-CARD
3/69 HI-LO
4/69 AIRPORT *2P*
4/69 HEARTS & SPADES
5/69 COLLEGE QUEENS *4P*
6/69 BUMPER POOL
7/69 TARGET POOL
8/69 MINI POOL
9/69 LARIAT *2P*
9/69 WILD WILD WEST *2P*
10/69 MIBS
11/69 SKIPPER *4P*
12/69 ROAD RACE
1/70 STOCK CAR
2/70 MINI CYCLE *2P*
2/70 POLO *4P*
3/70 FLIP-A-CARD
5/70 CARD TRIX
5/70 CRESCENDO *2P*
6/70 BASEBALL
7/70 GROOVY *4P*
8/70 BATTER UP
8/70 PSYCHEDELIC
9/70 SCUBA *2P*
10/70 AQUARIUS
11/70 SNOW QUEEN *4P*
12/70 SNOW DERBY *2P*
1/71 BRISTOL HILLS *2P*
1/71 DIMENSION
1/71 GALAXIE
2/71 2001
3/71 STAR TREK
4/71 NOW *4P*

5/71 CHALLENGER 2P	2/77 KICKER	10/85 ROCK 4P	7/76 SOUND STAGE 2P
5/71 EXTRA INNING	2/77 SOLAR CITY 2P	1/86 ROCK ENCORE 4P	9/76 JUKE BOX 4P
5/71 HOME RUN	3/77 BRONCO 4P	2/86 RAVEN 4P	1/77 STAMPEDE 2P
5/71 PLAY BALL	3/77 TEAM ONE	5/86 HOLLYWOOD HEAT 4P	2/77 RAWHIDE 4P
7/71 ROLLER COASTER 2P	5/77 JUNGLE QUEEN 4P	8/86 GENESIS 4P	6/77 DISCO 2P
8/71 CARD KING	5/77 MUSTANG 2P	10/86 GOLD WINGS 4P	8/77 PINBALL 4P
8/71 4 SQUARE	6/77 BIG HIT	2/87 MONTE CARLO 4P	12/77 STINGRAY 4P
9/71 SHERIFF 4P	6/77 LUCKY HAND	4/87 SPRING BREAK 4P	3/78 STARS 4P
10/71 ASTRO	7/77 LUCKY CARD	8/87 ARENA 4P	6/78 MEMORY LANE 4P
10/71 LAWMAN 2P	8/77 CENTIGRADE 37	10/87 VICTORY 4P	8/78 LECTRONAMO 4P
11/71 DROP-A-CARD	8/77 JET SPIN 4P	1/88 DIAMOND LADY 4P	10/78 WILD FYRE 4P
1/72 ORBIT 4P	8/77 JUNGLE PRINCESS 2P	3/88 TX-SECTOR 4P	11/78 NUGENT 4P
1/72 TEXAS RANGER	8/77 SUPER SPIN 2P		1/79 DRACULA 4P
2/72 OUTER-SPACE 2P	10/77 FIRE QUEEN 2P	**STERN ELECTRONICS**	3/79 TRIDENT 4P
3/72 FLYING CARPET	10/77 VULCAN 4P		6/79 HOT HAND 4P
3/72 POP-A-CARD	12/77 CLEOPATRA 4P	_(Chicago Coin changed its name in 1976)_	8/79 MAGIC 4P
4/72 SPACE ORBIT	12/77 PYRAMID 2P		9/79 METEOR 4P
5/72 KING ROCK 4P	78 CHARLIES ANGELS 4P	12/47 BERMUDA	1/80 GALAXY 4P
7/72 KING KOOL 2P	78 GOLDEN ARROW	1/48 CATALINA	3/80 ALI 4P
8/72 GRAND SLAM	78 NEPTUNE	3/48 TRINIDAD	3/80 BIG GAME 4P
8/72 WORLD SERIES	78 EYE OF THE TIGER 2P	4/48 SHANGHAI	5/80 SEAWITCH 4P
9/72 PLAY POOL	78 POSEIDEN	4/48 SPINBALL	6/80 CHEETAH 4P
12/72 JUNGLE 4P	78 ROCK STAR	7/48 CRAZY BALL	6/80 QUICKSILVER 4P
12/72 WILD LIFE 2P	78 BLUE NOTE	9/48 THRILL	9/80 STAR GAZER 4P
1/73 JUNGLE LIFE	2/78 SINBAD 4P	10/48 SALLY	10/80 FLIGHT 2000 4P
2/73 PRO FOOTBALL	3/78 STRANGE WORLD	11/48 TEMPTATION	11/80 NINE BALL 4P
5/73 JACK-IN-THE-BOX 4P	6/78 JOKER POKER 4P	12/48 HOLIDAY	2/81 FREEFALL 4P
5/73 JUNGLE KING 2P	8/78 CLOSE ENCOUNTERS 4P	1/49 GRAND AWARD	4/81 LIGHTNING 4P
5/73 TOP HAND	8/78 HIT THE DECK	2/49 MAJORS '49	8/81 SPLIT SECOND 4P
8/73 HIGH HAND	10/78 DRAGON 4P	4/49 SUPER HOCKEY	10/81 CATACOMB 4P
8/73 JUMPING JACK 2P	10/78 GEMINI 2P	6/49 CHAMPION	10/81 IRON MAIDEN 4P
8/73 TEN UP	79 TKO	7/49 GOLDEN GLOVES	12/81 VIPER 4P
12/73 HOT SHOT 4P	79 SPACE WALK 2P	8/49 FOOTBALL	1/82 DRAGONFIST 4P
12/73 KING PIN	2/79 SOLAR RIDE 4P	10/49 TAHITI	4/82 ORBITOR 1
12/73 PRO POOL	4/79 COUNT DOWN 4P	11/49 PIN BOWLER	10/84 LAZERLORD 4P
1/74 BIG SHOT 2P	6/79 PINBALL POOL 4P	11/50 FIGHTING IRISH	
2/74 SKY DIVE	8/79 GENIE 4P	12/50 PUNCHY	**UNITED**
4/74 BIG INDIAN 4P	8/79 TOTEM 4P	2/51 THE THING	
4/74 CAPTAIN CARD	10/79 INCREDIBLE HULK 4P	3/51 BOMBER	48 MONTERRAY
4/74 SKY JUMP	12/79 BUCK ROGERS 4P	12/51 KING PIN	48 RONDEVOO
6/74 BIG BRAVE 2P	80 ASTEROID ANNIE AND THE	3/52 WHIZZ KIDS	48 MAJOR LEAGUE BASEBALL
8/74 MAGNOTRON 4P	ALIENS	7/52 BIG HIT	48 PARADISE
9/74 DUOTRON 2P	2/80 ROLLER DISCO 4P	6/56 BLONDIE	48 PARADISE
9/74 FREE FALL	2/80 TORCH 4P	8/56 CAPRI	48 SUMMERTIME
9/74 TOP CARD	3/80 SPIDERMAN 4P	10/62 SUN VALLEY 2P	48 BLUE SKIES
10/74 ROYAL PAIR	5/80 PANTHERA 4P	10/63 FIRE CRACKER 2P	48 MOON GLOW
12/74 FAR OUT 2P	6/80 CIRCUS 4P	11/63 BRONCO 2P	48 SERENADE
75 WIZZARD	8/80 COUNTERFORCE 4P	1/64 ROYAL FLASH 2P	48 BABY FACE
1/75 ATLANTIS	10/80 JAMES BOND 4P	7/64 MUSTANG 2P	4/48 WISCONSIN
1/75 OUT OF SIGHT 4P	10/80 STAR RACE 4P	10/64 SOUTH PACIFIC	49 SHOW BOAT
3/75 SUPER SOCCER 4P	11/80 TIME LINE 4P	7/65 HULA-HULA 2P	49 RAMONA
4/75 EL DURADO	1/81 FORCE II 4P	8/66 FESTIVAL 4P	49 CAROLINA
4/75 PIN UP	3/81 PINK PANTHER 4P	8/66 KICKER	49 AQUACADE
4/75 SOCCER 2P	4/81 MARS 4P	1/67 BEATNIKS 2P	49 OKLAHOMA
7/75 FAST DRAW 4P	7/81 VOLCANO 4P	7/67 TWINKY 2P	49 PINCH HITTER
7/75 QUICK DRAW 2P	10/81 BLACK HOLE 4P	4/68 GUN SMOKE 2P	49 TAMPICO
8/75 SPIN OUT	82 ECLIPSE 4P	6/68 STAGE COACH 4P	49 UTAH
8/75 TIGER	2/82 HAUNTED HOUSE 4P	10/68 PLAYTIME 2P	50 ARIZONA
10/75 TOP SCORE 2P	4/82 DEVILS DARE 4P	1/69 PIRATE GOLD	50 RED SHOES
10/75 300 4P	5/82 CAVEMAN 4P	6/69 ASTRONAUT 2P	
11/75 ABRA CA DABRA	8/82 ROCKY 4P	8/69 MOON SHOT 4P	**VALLEY**
11/75 LUCKY STRIKE	8/82 SPIRT 4P	9/69 ACTION	
1/76 GOLD STRIKE	9/82 PUNK 4P	1/70 BIG FLIPPER 2P	78 SPECTRA IV 4P
3/76 BANK SHOT	11/82 STRIKER 4P	1/70 COWBOY 4P	
3/76 PIONEER 2P	83 GOIN' NUTS 4P	8/71 HIGH SCORE POOL 2P	**VENTURE LINE**
3/76 SPIRIT OF 76 4P	2/83 KRULL 4P	6/72 CASINO 4P	
3/76 SPOT POOL	3/83 Q-BERTS QUEST 4P	4/73 HEE HAW 4P	78 JOKER'S WILD 4P
3/76 SURE SHOT	4/83 ROYAL FLUSH DELUX 4P	7/73 RIVIERA 4P	
4/76 ROYAL FLUSH 4P	4/83 SUPER ORBIT 4P	3/74 DOLPHIN 2P	**VIZA MANUFACTURING**
6/76 SHIP AHOY	8/83 AMAZON HUNT 4P	4/74 SHOWTIME 4P	
7/76 BUCCANEER	10/83 RACK 'EM UP 4P	8/74 HI-FLYER 2P	8/78 FABULOUS '50S 2P
8/76 CARD WHIZ 2P	12/83 READY, AIM, FIRE 4P	10/74 SKY RIDER 4P	10/78 WAR 2P
8/76 NEW YORK 2P	2/84 JACKS TO OPEN 4P	11/74 GIN	
10/76 SURF CHAMP 4P	4/84 THE GAMES 4P	1/75 OLYMPICS 2P	**WICO**
10/76 VOLLEY	6/84 ALIEN STAR 4P	1/75 SUPER STAR 4P	
11/76 HIGH SEAS	9/84 TOUCHDOWN 4P	3/75 TOP TEN 2P	10/84 AF-TOR 4P
11/76 SURFER 2P	10/84 EL DORADO 4P	4/75 GOLD RECORD 4P	
11/76 TARGET ALPHA 4P	2/85 ICE FEVER 4P	6/75 RED BARON 2P	**WILLIAMS**
77 GRIDIRON 2P	5/85 CHICAGO CUBS TRIPLE PLAY 4P	7/75 BLUE MAX 4P	
1/77 CANADA DRY 4P	7/85 BOUNTY HUNTER 4P	2/76 HOLLYWOOD 2P	12/47 SUNNY
1/77 JACKS OPEN	9/85 TAG TEAM PINBALL 4P	4/76 CINEMA 4P	1/48 STORMY
			2/48 TENNESSEE
			3/48 VIRGINIA
			4/48 YANKS

Date	Machine
6/48	DEW-WA-DITTY
8/48	GIZMO
9/48	SPEEDWAY
9/48	RAINBOW
10/48	SARATOGA
11/48	EL PASO
1/49	TUSCON
2/49	DALLAS
2/49	ST. LOUIS
4/49	MARYLAND
5/49	BOSTON
9/49	FRESHIE
11/49	DE-ICER
2/50	DREAMY
5/50	SWEETHEART
7/50	GEORGIA
9/50	PINKY
10/50	RAG MOP
2/51	SHOO SHOO
3/51	CONTROL TOWER
5/51	HARVEY
6/51	HAYBURNERS
6/51	SNOOKS
8/51	JALOPY
9/51	SPARK PLUG
11/51	ARCADE
11/51	SEA JOCKEY
11/51	SHOOT THE MOON
12/51	HORSE SHOES
52	ALL AMERICAN QUARTERBACK
1/52	HORSE FEATHERS
1/52	SWEEPSTAKES
1/52	8 BALL
2/52	SPORTSMAN
3/52	SLUGFEST
4/52	MAJORETTES
5/52	DOMINO
5/52	OLYMPICS
6/52	CARAVAN
6/52	HANDICAP
8/52	PARATROOPER
9/52	HONG KONG
10/52	4 CORNERS
11/52	DISK JOCKEY
12/52	TWENTY GRAND
2/53	SILVER SKATES
3/53	STARLITE
4/53	TIMES SQUARE
6/53	FAIRWAY
7/53	PALISADES
8/53	GRAND CHAMPION
9/53	C O D
10/53	ARMY NAVY
10/53	GUN CLUB
11/53	STRUGGLE BUGGIES
12/53	DEALER
12/53	LAZY-Q
12/53	NINE SISTERS
1/54	THUNDERBIRD
2/54	SKYWAY
3/54	SCREAMO
5/54	BIG BEN
6/54	DAFFY DERBY
7/54	CUE TEE
7/54	STAR POOL
8/54	COLORS
11/54	LULU
12/54	SPIT FIRE
3/55	PETER PAN
3/55	RACE THE CLOCK 4P
4/55	WONDERLAND
5/55	BAND WAGON 4P
5/55	SMOKE SIGNAL
5/55	THREE DEUCES
8/55	CIRCUS WAGON 2P
8/55	JOLLY JOKER
8/55	REGATTA
8/55	SNAFU
1/56	TIM-BUC-TU
4/56	PICCADILLY 2P
5/56	HOT DIGGITY
5/56	SURF RIDER
6/56	SUPER SCORE
8/56	FUN HOUSE 4P
9/56	PERKY
9/56	STARFIRE
10/56	SHAMROCK 2P
12/56	CUE BALL
57	ADD-A-BALL
1/57	GAY PAREE 4P
2/57	ARROW HEAD
8/57	NAPLES 2P
9/57	KINGS
9/57	RENO
10/57	STEEPLECHASE
11/57	JIG SAW
2/58	TOP HAT 2P
3/58	KICK OFF
6/58	SATELLITE
7/58	TURF CHAMP
7/58	4 STAR
8/58	CASINO
9/58	GUSHER
11/58	CLUB HOUSE
11/58	3-D
1/59	TIC-TAC-TOE
2/59	GOLDEN BELLS
2/59	SPOT POOL
4/59	CROSSWORD
11/59	ROCKET
12/59	FIESTA 2P
1/60	GOLDEN GLOVES
2/60	21
4/60	NAGS
5/60	SERENADE 2P
6/60	DARTS
6/60	VIKING 2P
7/60	JUNGLE
8/60	MUSIC MAN 4P
11/60	BLACK JACK
12/60	MAGIC CLOCK 2P
1/61	BOBO
2/61	CARAVELLE 4P
3/61	HIGHWAYS
5/61	HOLLYWOOD 2P
6/61	TEN SPOT
8/61	DOUBLE BARREL 2P
9/61	SKILL BALL
10/61	RESERVE
11/61	KISMET 4P
12/61	METRO
12/61	SPACE SHIP
2/62	JOLLY JOKERS
2/62	3 COINS
5/62	COQUETTE 2P
6/62	TRADE WINDS
7/62	FRIENDSHIP 7
8/62	VALIANT 2P
9/62	KING PIN 2P
10/62	MARDI GRAS 4P
10/62	VAGABOND
12/62	4 ROSES
1/63	TOM TOM 2P
2/63	BIG DEAL
4/63	JUMPIN' JACKS 2P
5/63	SWING TIME
6/63	SKILL POOL
8/63	EL TORO 2P
9/63	BIG DADDY
10/63	MERRY WIDOW 4P
12/63	BEAT THE CLOCK
2/64	OH BOY 2P
3/64	SOCCER 2P
4/64	PALOOKA
5/64	SAN FRANCISCO 2P
7/64	HEAT WAVE
8/64	STOP N GO 2P
9/64	RIVER BOAT
10/64	WHOOPEE 4P
12/64	WING DING
12/64	ZIG ZAG
1/65	PRETTY BABY 2P
3/65	ALPINE CLUB
3/65	SKI CLUB
4/65	EAGER BEAVER 2P
5/65	MOULIN ROUGE
6/65	POT-O' GOLD 2P
8/65	LUCKY STRIKE
9/65	BIG CHIEF 4P
11/65	BOWL-A-STRIKE
12/65	TEACHERS PET
1/66	8 BALL 2P
3/66	FULL HOUSE
4/66	TOP HAND
5/66	A-GO-GO 4P
8/66	BIG STRIKE
10/66	HOT LINE
11/66	CASANOVA 2P
1/67	MAGIC CITY
2/67	MAGIC TOWN
3/67	SHANGRI-LA 4P
5/67	BLAST OFF
6/67	APOLLO
8/67	LUNAR SHOT
9/67	BEAT TIME 2P
10/67	DERBY DAY 2P
11/67	TOUCHDOWN
12/67	KICK OFF
2/68	DING DONG
2/68	JOLLY ROGER 4P
2/68	SMARTY
3/68	LADY LUCK 2P
5/68	DAFFIE
6/68	STUDENT PRINCE 4P
8/68	DOOZIE
8/68	HAYBURNERS II 2P
10/68	PIT STOP 2P
11/68	CUE-T
1/69	CABARET 4P
2/69	MISS-O
4/69	POST TIME
5/69	SUSPENSE 2P
6/69	SMART SET 4P
9/69	PADDOCK
10/69	EXPO 2P
10/69	GRIDIRON 2P
10/69	ROTO 2P
12/69	SET UP
12/69	SEVEN UP
1/70	GAY 90'S 4P
3/70	4 ACES 2P
4/70	JIVE TIME
4/70	ROCK N ROLL
8/70	ACES & KINGS 4P
9/70	STRIKE ZONE 2P
10/70	STRAIGHT FLUSH
10/70	3 JOKERS
1/71	DIPSY DOODLE 4P
2/71	SOLIDS N STRIPES 2P
3/71	LOVE BUG
4/71	DOODLE BUG
4/71	GOLD RUSH 4P
4/71	JACKPOT 4P
8/71	KLONDIKE
8/71	PLANETS 2P
8/71	YUKON
8/71	ZODIAC 2P
1/72	STARDUST 4P
2/72	OLYMPIC HOCKEY 2P
2/72	WINNER 2P
3/72	GRANADA
5/72	SPANISH EYES
8/72	HONEY 4P
9/72	SUPER STAR
12/72	BIG STAR
12/72	FAN-TAS-TIC 4P
1/73	SWINGER 2P
2/73	SUMMER TIME
2/73	TRAVEL TIME
5/73	FUN-FEST 4P
5/73	TROPIC FUN
6/73	GULFSTREAM
9/73	DARLING 2P
9/73	JUBILEE 4P
74	TRAMWAY 4P
1/74	OXO 4P
2/74	STAR ACTION
3/74	TRIPLE ACTION
6/74	DEALERS CHOICE 4P
7/74	SKYLAB
7/74	SPACELAB
10/74	STRATO-FLITE 4P
11/74	HIGH ACE 4P
11/74	SUPER-FLITE 2P
12/74	LUCKY ACE
3/75	STAR POOL 4P
4/75	SATIN DOLL 2P
5/75	BIG BEN
7/75	PAT HAND 4P
9/75	BLACK GOLD
9/75	TRIPLE STRIKE
12/75	LITTLE CHIEF 4P
76	VALENCIA 4P
1/76	TOLEDO 2P
5/76	SPACE MISSION 4P
7/76	SPACE ODYSSEY 2P
11/76	AZTEC 4P
11/76	BLUE CHIP
12/76	GRAND PRIX 4P
77	ARGOSY 4P
77	RANCHO 2P
4/77	LIBERTY BELL 2P
5/77	BIG DEAL 4P
10/77	WILD CARD
11/77	HOT TIP 4P
3/78	LUCKY SEVEN 4P
5/78	WORLD CUP 4P
6/78	CONTACT 4P
6/78	DISCO FEVER 4P
12/78	PHOENIX 4P
12/78	POKERINO 4P
1/79	FLASH 4P
5/79	STELLAR WARS
8/79	TRI ZONE 4P
9/79	TIME WARP 4P
12/79	GORGAR 4P
12/79	LASER BALL 4P
3/80	FIREPOWER 4P
10/80	BLACKOUT 4P
10/80	SCORPION 4P
11/80	ALIEN POKER 4P
11/80	ALGAR 4P
12/80	BLACK KNIGHT 4P
3/81	JUNGLE LORD 4P
7/81	PHARAOH 4P
10/81	SOLAR FIRE 4P
11/81	BARRACORA 4P
82	VARKON 2P
7/82	COSMIC GUNFIGHT 4P
11/82	DEFENDER 2P
11/82	TIME FANTASY 2P
83	THUNDERBALL 4P
1/83	WARLOK 4P
10/83	JOUST 2P
1/84	FIREPOWER II 4P
3/84	LASER CUE 4P
8/84	STARLIGHT 4P
8/84	STAR LIGHT 4P
10/84	SPACE SHUTTLE 4P
10/84	GRIDIRON 2P
10/84	SPACE SHUTTLE 4P
3/85	SORCERER 4P
9/85	COMET 4P
2/86	HIGH SPEED 4P
7/86	GRAND LIZARD 4P
8/86	ROAD KINGS 4P
10/86	PINBOT 4P
2/87	MILLIONAIRE 4P
3/87	F-14 TOMCAT 4P
6/87	FIRE 4P
9/87	FIRE CHAMPAGNE EDITION 4P
10/87	BIG GUNS 4P
1/88	SPACE STATION 4P
3/88	CYCLONE 4P

ACKNOWLEDGEMENTS

The authors and publishers of this book would like to thank the following for their help in producing this book and for providing pictures and machines for photography:

Allied Leisure; Associated Leisure/David Wilcox; Atari; Atlas Photography; Laura at Bally; Rob Berk/Pinball Expo' USA; *The Billboard;* John Bilotta; Brent Leisure; Dick Bueschel; Chicago Coin Co. (Stern Electronics); Tony Clarke; Philip Crowe; Data East; Deith Leisure; Dave Dutton; Electracoin; Exhibit Supply Co.; Paul Forrester; Philip Fuller; John Gibson; Harry Hoppe Corp.; Ad Jonker; Steve Kordek at Williams; Stanley Knoll; Dan Kramer; Mills Novelty Co.; Mike Pacak flyers; Christopher Pearce; The Pinball Owners Association (GB); Gil Pollack at Premier; Ed Smith; Tim Sharp; Dave Snook/ *The Coin Slot;* Andrew Sydenham; Keith Temple; Kem Thorn; Bob Thomson; David Wright; Zaccaria.

Special thanks are due to "the Big Three" — Bally, Gottlieb/Premier, and Williams — for permission to reproduce advertising material; and particularly to Jean-Pierre Cuvier, who provided images on the following pages:

(a = above, b = below, l = left, r = right)

pp 34b, 36, 37, 41, 42, 43b, 44b, 45, 49, 51, 55, 57, 65l, 69l, 89r.